I Am His

UNDERSTANDING YOUR IDENTITY THROUGH JESUS CHRIST

I Am His

UNDERSTANDING YOUR IDENTITY THROUGH JESUS CHRIST

MARK D. LYMAN
SARAH LYMAN SMITH

CFI
An imprint of Cedar Fort, Inc.
Springville, Utah

ISBN 13: 978-1-4621-4515-7

Published by CFI, an imprint of Cedar Fort, Inc.
2373 W. 700 S., Suite 100, Springville, UT 84663
Distributed by Cedar Fort, Inc., www.cedarfort.com

Library of Congress Control Number: 2023934885

Cover design by Shawnda Craig

Edited and Typeset by Liz Kazandzhy

Printed in the United States of America

10 9 8 7 6 5 4 3 2 1

Printed on acid-free paper

This book is dedicated to our mothers,
who do so much to teach us who we are.

Other Books by the Authors

Love, Kynra
by Mark Lyman

Contents

"It is a serious thing to live in a society of possible gods and goddesses, to remember that the dullest and most uninteresting person you talk to may one day be a creature which, if you saw it now, you would be strongly tempted to worship. . . . There are no ordinary people. You have never talked to a mere mortal. . . . Next to the blessed sacrament itself, your neighbor is the holiest object presented to your senses."

–*C. S. Lewis*[1]

1. C. S. Lewis, *The Weight of Glory* (New York: Macmillan, 1949), 45.

Introduction

Sarah: After about six months as a missionary in Denmark, my companion and I were boarding a train to cross the countryside. I knew I'd be riding for hours, so I prayed to sit by someone talkative and maybe even willing to visit about faith. I'd rarely met a Dane who believed in God, though they often admitted to believing in "something bigger"—and usually wanted to leave it at that.

Fortunately, I found a talker. As we chatted, I learned he had spent significant time in Denmark but was from Australia, so we continued our conversation in English. Although not religious, like many Danes he also believed in "something bigger." Unlike others, however, he was willing to explain why.

He said that some years ago he was planning a trip abroad and gathering the required documents. When he received his birth certificate in the mail, he felt its significance and simultaneously felt its *insignificance.* He somehow knew that this identifying record could not capture his true self. He sensed he was more than just another human being—born, named, and officially logged.

With both hands pointing at his heart, he said, "There is something in me that a certificate cannot signify. Deep inside, I am something greater than any piece of paper."

I was touched by his emotion and intuitive understanding.

He *is* "something greater." He *comes from* "something bigger." He is not only his parents' child or a citizen of Australia, he is a son of God and a son of God's covenant. In fact, before his birth, with faith he chose the Father's plan and the discipleship of Jesus Christ.

Our sacred, eternal identity comes through the Savior. Ultimately and most simply put, we are His.

His earthly mother and father had not taught him these things, but his Father in Heaven had. "The Spirit enlighteneth every man through the world, that hearkeneth to the voice of the Spirit" (Doctrine and Covenants 84:46).

***

Because we are God's literal children, we intuitively and correctly sense that our identity is special and important and needs to be understood by ourselves and others. President Russell M. Nelson has carefully and clearly taught this truth. Sister Bonnie H. Cordon said that as he called her to serve as the Young Women General President, "he asked a question that still echoes in my heart, 'Bonnie, what's the most important thing the [youth] need to know?' I pondered for a moment and said, 'they need to know who they are.' 'YES!' he exclaimed, 'and they need to know their purpose.'"[1]

This book is a Christian-based look at identity. As members of The Church of Jesus Christ of Latter-day Saints, references to "the Church" are references to our faith. We hope that anyone seeking to understand humankind's identity will try the perspective of faith. Science offers important insights regarding origin, and so does religion. Some people might dismiss both and seek their own way forward. But through faith in Jesus Christ, we have found both logical and faith-filled answers to questions about our origin, purpose, and destiny.

President Nelson taught, "It is important to know who you are and who you may become. It is more important than what you do, vital as your work is." He then adds this caution: "I emphasize this because some people on life's journey forget who they really are and

---

1. Bonnie H. Cordon, "Come unto Christ and Don't Come Alone," *Liahona*, Nov. 2021, 10.

what is really important. Without sure identity and priority, blessings that matter most are at the mercy of things that matter least."[2]

Identity has been increasingly discussed by the leadership of the Church recently. Use of the word *identity* during the Church's semiannual general conference has rapidly increased during the past several decades, with use per 1 million words surging from just nine in the 1960s, to forty-eight in the 1990s, to ninety-seven so far in this decade (January 2020 through April 2022), a greater than tenfold rise over the last half century.[3] This growing need to understand, act on, and teach divine identity is a prophetic priority.

The reasons are all around us. Secularism is ever stronger and more alluring, leading both youth and adults to drift into false identities influenced by worldly trends, violent video games, glorified immorality, and the virtual world of social media. False identities can result in apathy, confusion, anxiety, and depression and even lead to self-harm and suicide. Body image disorders, violence, addictions, and faith crises are some of the manifestations of this growing problem.

As children of God, we need to know clearly who we are and what our divine purpose is. If we don't know or accept our divine identity, we are more vulnerable to the confusing and destructive messages of the adversary. President Nelson and other Church leaders repeatedly point to understanding divine identity as a powerful solution.

Elder Tad R. Callister related the following: "At a recent training session for General Authorities, the question was asked: 'How can we help those struggling with pornography?' Elder Russell M. Nelson stood and replied, 'Teach them their identity and their purpose.' That answer resonated with me, not only as a response to that specific question but as an appropriate response to most of the challenges we face in life."[4]

As we try to plant eternal gospel truth deep in our hearts and in the hearts of our loved ones, few teachings are more powerful than

---

2. Russell M. Nelson, "Identity, Priority, and Blessings," *Ensign*, Aug. 2001, 6.
3. LDS General Conference Corpus, "identity," https://www.lds-general-conference.org, accessed Jan. 23, 2023.
4. Tad R. Callister, "Our Identity and Our Destiny" (Brigham Young University devotional, Aug. 14, 2012), 1, speeches.byu.edu.

divine identity. Elder José A. Teixeira said, "Knowing who you are changes what you feel and what you do. Understanding who you truly are better prepares you to recognize and remember your way back to your heavenly home and yearn to be there."[5]

We have done our best to present this important topic logically, simply, and accurately. However, we are aware that the concepts of divine identity can be expanded and much better explained by others. We hope this conversation continues to happen in other books, forums, articles, and research.

Although we are members of the Church, we are not authorities in the Church. We are not experts on identity. We struggle with these concepts personally and wrote this book seeking additional knowledge and faith to guide our lives. In other words, this book is a representation of our imperfect understanding, not an official representation of the teachings of The Church of Jesus Christ of Latter-day Saints.

We hope the reader will listen carefully to their own inspired thoughts and feelings and record them, whether or not those thoughts are related to the book's content. Ultimately, we recognize that the prophets of God and the Holy Ghost are the authoritative teachers of restored gospel truth for us individually and as a whole.

5. José A. Teixeira, "Remember Your Way Back Home," *Liahona*, May 2021, 92.

1

I Am His

The King of love my Shepherd is,
Whose goodness faileth never;
I nothing lack if I am His
And He is mine forever.
—Henry W. Baker[6]

Where did we come from? Why are we here? Where will we go after we die? As human beings, we often struggle to develop and clarify our own identity. Even the prophets Moses and David asked God, "Who am I?" (see Exodus 3:11 and 2 Samuel 7:18).

In the restored gospel, we might feel a bit self-assured because we know those answers. Or do we?

At a fireside in Las Vegas, Nevada, speaking to young adults, President Russell M. Nelson made a striking statement about our identity: "One of the most important things you need to learn in life is to know who you really are. When you begin to catch even a glimpse

6. Henry W. Baker, "The King of Love," *Masterpieces of Religious Verse* (New York: Harper, 1948), no. 783.

of how your Heavenly Father sees you and what He is counting on you to do for Him, your life will never be the same."[7]

What exactly does he mean by this remarkable statement? Don't we as members of the restored Church already know enough about who we "really are"?

We must have more to learn about this crucial topic if a prophet is telling covenant members of the Church that we might lack even a "glimpse" of how our Heavenly Father sees us and what He is counting on us to do, and promising that our lives will never be the same if only we will catch this "glimpse."

As followers of Christ's restored gospel, of course we know many meaningful details about our divine identity, such as "I am a child of God." President Nelson said, "I fear that you may have heard this truth so often that it sounds more like a slogan than divine truth."[8] Are we so changed by our understanding of divine identity that our lives will "never be the same"? Or do we view ourselves day to day with a more worldly identity?

Whatever understanding we have, remembering our divine identity is not easy. We live in an increasingly secular world which, despite good intentions and powerful research, does not comprehend who we really are. In fact, the world regularly teaches that we are here by random accident and, by implication, without divine identity or eternal purpose.

So, how can we better understand and internalize our divine identity?

Jesus gives us the perfect example. He comprehended and accepted His identity in the premortal world and throughout His mortal life. He therefore received all our Heavenly Father wanted to give Him. He became all He was meant to become. He is our exemplar in this way, as in every good and great way. In fact, He literally is "the way" (John 14:6).

In contrast, Lucifer gives us an example of the dangers of failing to understand and accept who we are. Lucifer was also created and

---

7. Russell M. Nelson, quoted in "President Russell M. Nelson Speaks to Millennials about Being Happy," *Church News*, Feb. 23, 2018.

8. Russell M. Nelson, "Choices for Eternity,"

destined with divine purpose. But he did not desire to identify himself with God. Instead, he chose to abandon his true identity and create for himself an identity outside of and in opposition to God's plan.

Satan desired to *redefine* himself. Maybe "redefining" yourself does not sound so bad. Yet we can't improve on or add to God's plans or designs for us. If we try to change our divine identity, all of which comes through Jesus Christ, we will only subtract from our divine destiny, and we may even destroy our limitless potential. Literally everything is at stake!

Sister Camille N. Johnson said:

> I testify that the Savior is "the author and finisher of our faith." Will you invite Him to be the author and finisher of your story?
>
> He knows the beginning from the end. He was the Creator of heaven and earth. He wants us to return home to Him and our Heavenly Father. He has everything invested in us and wants us to succeed. . . .
>
> Why do we want the Savior to be the author and the finisher of our stories? Because He knows our potential perfectly, He will take us to places we never imagined ourselves. He may make us a David or an Esther. He will stretch us and refine us to be more like Him.[9]

So, what is the simple, clear answer to who we are?

We are His.

Without the assurance of a Savior and Redeemer, we would not have been born to our parents in heaven. Without Jehovah, we would not have been born on earth. Without Jesus Christ, we cannot be reborn into immortality and eternal life.

We come from Him and through Him. He is the way, the truth and the life (see John 14:6).

Worldwide and through all time, we are equal in our most important identity: "I am His."

That means everything and forever. In fact, understanding the scope of our divine identity is so all-encompassing that the power of this concept is hard to comprehend. Perhaps an even imperfect analogy will help.

---

9. Camille N. Johnson, "Invite Christ to Author Your Story," *Liahona*, Nov. 2021, 80.

Rocket ships, complex and beautiful, are designed for great heights, lofty purposes, and important missions. The rocket is designed by some of the brightest, most creative, and most disciplined minds. Likewise, those who are given stewardship to pilot rockets are elite in their physical and intellectual ability and also in their trustworthiness. The rocket ship is a special, extremely precious, and highly engineered vehicle. If all goes well, it will rise above the earth itself, transcend the vastness of space, and do a marvelous and wonderful work.

Like a perfectly performing rocket ship, Jesus accepts His divine role and executes His special mission completely and with exactness. Because He humbly fulfills His great task, He soars to unimaginable heights, and we breathlessly adore, admire, and worship Him. He consequently puts Himself in a position to do all His Designer created Him to do: love without limits, set the perfect example, teach with stunning clarity and power, create worlds without number, save and redeem us from death and sin, and judge us with perfect understanding, justice, and mercy. Jesus Christ fulfills with faithfulness every part of His transcendent identity.

A rocket ship is so special that it is hard to imagine anyone deciding to use it for something other than its designed purpose. Just try. It's not easy to visualize that.

Maybe start by imagining a massive rocket: newly created, fully fueled, gleaming in the sun on the launch pad, with expert astronauts in place, ready to gloriously blast off into space to perform a vital mission. Then, for unexplained reasons, the mission is abandoned. The owner of the rocket ship tells the astronauts to unstrap, come down, take off their suits, and return home. Confusion results. Then the rocket ship is coarsely cut in half and refurbished into a trinket store, never to rise above the world or fulfill its designed purposes.

This might briefly be amusing at best, but ultimately such changes in the true identity of the rocket ship would be short-sighted, sad, and possibly harmful.

If God is the tree, then denying our divine relationship to Him is like cutting off the branch we are sitting on. When we fail to recognize who we are and fail to do what we are designed to do, the results are short-sighted, harmful, and sad in the most consequential, profound, and eternal ways.

Elder Dale G. Renlund said, "The third truth in the opening paragraph of the Young Women theme is that we have 'a divine nature.' This is intrinsic to who we are. It is spiritually 'genetic,' inherited from our heavenly parents, and requires no effort on our part. This is our most important identity, regardless of how else we choose to identify ourselves."[10]

Satan takes misuse of his own design to a new, dark low. He descends far beneath the idea of a trinket store. His actions are similar to deciding to use the rocket as a means to control others, or as a weapon to cause damage, maim, kill, and even destroy an entire world.

Like Jesus, we are the children of God, created in His image and sent forth with divine purpose and destiny. Like Jesus, our challenge is to fully realize and embrace our destiny. Following His example of understanding and realizing our divine identity is among the most life-changing things we can do.

Sister Michelle D. Craig said, "Perhaps the most important things for us to see clearly are who God is and who we really are—sons and daughters of heavenly parents, with a 'divine nature and eternal destiny.' Ask God to reveal these truths to you, along with how He feels about you. The more you understand your true identity and purpose, soul deep, the more it will influence everything in your life."[11]

As people of faith, we might feel that we already know our identity and are comfortable with our understanding of who we are, why we are here, and where we will go after we die. However, let's take another look. Let's see if we can find greater understanding in this area of promised clarity and power. Maybe we can learn specific ways to act on what we know. Perhaps we can catch that "glimpse" of who we really are, and if we do, our lives will never be the same.

That's a prophetic promise.

---

10. Dale G. Renlund, "Your Divine Nature and Eternal Destiny," *Liahona*, May 2022, 75.

11. Michelle D. Craig, "Eyes to See," *Ensign* or *Liahona*, Nov. 2020, 15–16.

2

Divine Identity through Our Status as Children

Please come closer so you will know
Just who my child is and what I see
When those sweet eyes stare back at me
—*Gary Shulman*[12]

Our identity can be traced to our origins. So, it makes sense that ancient and modern prophets teach that our divine identity is based in our origins as children. We are (1) *children* of heavenly parents, (2) *children* of the covenant, and (3) *children* of Jesus Christ. These are our most important origins and identities. There is no greater heritage, and therefore no greater identity, than the birthrights we receive as children in these three divine ways.

President Russell M. Nelson said, "First and foremost, you are a child of God. Second, as a member of the Church, you are a child of the covenant. And third, you are a disciple of Jesus Christ. Tonight, I

12. Gary Shulman, "Come Touch His Cheek," Poetry Nation, accessed Jan. 24, 2023, https://www.poetrynation.com/poems/come-touch-his-cheek/.

plead with you not to replace these three paramount and unchanging identifiers with any others, because doing so could stymie your progress or pigeonhole you in a stereotype that could potentially thwart your eternal progression."[13]

God's children are supremely precious to Him. Some of His most tender actions and words are about His children. "Suffer little children, and forbid them not, to come unto me: for of such is the kingdom of heaven" (Matthew 19:4). As His children, we are His "work" and "glory" (Moses 1:39).

First, we are children of heavenly parents. We carry within our souls their divine DNA. In Acts we read, "We are the offspring of God" (Acts 17:29). As President Nelson said, "We are sons and daughters of Almighty God. He is our Father. We are His children. Our divine inheritance is the magnificence of humankind."[14]

We are the children of the covenant as well. During the visit of Jesus Christ to the people on the American continent, He said, "The Father having raised me up unto you first, and sent me to bless you in turning away every one of you from his iniquities; and this because *ye are the children of the covenant*" (3 Nephi 20:25-26; emphasis added).

We are also the children of Christ. Through the Atonement of Jesus Christ, we become "his seed" (Mosiah 15:11), are "born again" (John, 3:3), and are "begotten" of Him (Doctrine and Covenants 76:24). Though we are born spiritually to heavenly parents and physically to our earthly parents, because of Christ's Atonement, we are reborn of Him.

The concept of children repeatedly stands out. When teaching of divine identity, prophets also use words related to children and birth, including seed, offspring, daughter, son, begotten, birthright, and born. In understanding identity, the emphasis on our status as children clearly means something significant.

A common definition of the word *child* is a descendant. Although *child* has other meanings, this definition is the most important in

---

13. Russell M. Nelson, "Choices for Eternity" (worldwide devotional for young adults, May 15, 2022), broadcasts.ChurchofJesusChrist.org.

14. Russell M. Nelson, "Your Body: A Magnificent Gift to Cherish," *New Era*, Aug. 2019, 2.

understanding identity. To be a descendant implies heritage, potential, and inheritance. Our divine identity is primarily defined by our divine parentage. We are offspring, not accidents.

On one level, this might appear obvious. Every day we see examples of identity through our status as children. We carry the names and characteristics of our parents. Hummingbirds come from hummingbirds, oak trees from oak trees, and oysters from oysters. Parents and children are the pattern of life, ever-present and constant.

President Boyd K. Packer teaches this significance in the following story:

> Some years ago I returned home to find our little children . . . had discovered some newly hatched chicks under the manger in the barn. . . . As our little girl held one of them, I said in a teasing way, "That will make a nice watchdog when it grows up, won't it?" She looked at me quizzically, as if I didn't know much.
>
> So I changed my approach: "It won't be a watchdog, will it?" She shook her head, "No, Daddy." Then I added, "It will be a nice riding horse."
>
> She wrinkled up her nose and gave me that "Oh, Dad!" look. For even a four-year-old knows that a chick will not be a dog, nor a horse, nor even a turkey. It will be a chicken. It will follow the pattern of its parentage. She knew that without having had a course in genetics, without a lesson or a lecture. . . .
>
> We may now be young in our progression—juvenile, even infantile, compared with Him. Nevertheless, in the eternities to come, if we are worthy, we may be like unto Him.[15]

The spiritual "pattern of parentage," as it pertains to the children of God, means everything. We have the potential to receive all and become all *because we are His children*. In this one sense, our divine identity is clearly our most meaningful identity.

As part of our identity, we are carefully designed and endowed to reach this destiny. As daughters of heavenly parents, girls and women are designed and destined to become like Heavenly Mother. As their sons, boys and men are designed and destined to become like Heavenly Father.

---

15. Boyd K. Packer, "The Pattern of Our Parentage," *Ensign*, Nov. 1984, 67.

Elder Tad R. Callister said, "As we better understand our potential destiny, our level of self-worth and confidence and motivation is greatly heightened."[16]

In a more earthly way, the idea of "identity through parentage" can be a bit scary. We are all born to imperfect humans. Some of us even come from family situations that are riddled with tragedy, corruption, abuse, poor judgement, or various sins. No matter who we are, we inherit weaknesses from our imperfect earthly parents.

We can take comfort in knowing that weakness, adversity, and opposition in mortality do not define us—they simply define our mortal condition. Weakness is a constant part of our situation on earth. Yet if we identify with our weakness, we will confuse who we are and wander from eternal truth.[17]

Elder Dieter F. Uchtdorf said:

> The Savior's infinite Atonement completely changes the way we may view our transgressions and imperfections. Instead of dwelling on them and feeling irredeemable or hopeless, we can learn from them and feel hopeful. The gift of repentance is the process that allows us to leave our sins behind and emerge a new creature.
>
> Because of Jesus Christ, *our failures do not have to define us. They can refine us.*
>
> Like a musician rehearsing scales, we can see our missteps, flaws, and sins as opportunities for greater self-awareness, deeper and more honest love for others, and refinement through repentance.
>
> If we repent, mistakes do not disqualify us. They are part of our progress.[18]

Likewise, we are not defined by abuse. Speaking to those who have been abused, Elder Patrick Kearon said:

> God does not now see, nor has He ever seen, you as someone to be despised. Whatever has happened to you, He is not ashamed of you or disappointed in you. He loves you in a way you have yet

---

16. Tad R. Callister, "Our Identity and Our Destiny" (Brigham Young University devotional, Aug. 14, 2012), 9, speeches.byu.edu.

17. See Appendix C.

18. Dieter F. Uchtdorf, "God Among Us," *Liahona*, May 2021, 8–9; emphasis added.

> to discover. And you will discover it as you trust in His promises and as you learn to believe Him when He says you are "precious in [His] sight."
>
> You are not defined by these terrible things that have been done to you. You are, in glorious truth, defined by your eternally existing identity as a son or daughter of God and by your Creator's perfect, infinite love and invitation to whole and complete healing.[19]

Again, it is important to note the spiritual emphasis of the word *children* in teachings on identity. Whatever weakness we inherit from our earthly parents or whatever happens to us does not define us eternally—it is simply part of our mortal circumstance. As Elder Gerrit W. Gong taught, "Genetics and family patterns influence but do not determine us."[20] Our eternal identity comes from our heavenly parents, through our Savior and Redeemer, and the covenants of God.

Many of us are born on earth to noble and wise parents who love and cherish us. We inherit weakness, but we also inherit strength from them. We honor them as we magnify the good we receive from them and strive through Jesus Christ to overcome our weakness. If we are fortunate to be born to parents on earth who live meekly and faithfully as God intended, we inherit much spiritual strength from them as well.

Our spiritual births (as children of heavenly parents, of Christ, and of the covenant) are of supreme importance to our identity. These spiritual beginnings are divinely designed and closely related. In subsequent chapters, we will review in greater depth our status as children of Christ and as children of the covenants of God.

To explore in more depth the significance of our identity as children, we now briefly focus on our spiritual birth to heavenly parents.

Before our spiritual birth to heavenly parents, we existed as intelligences, a lesser condition we don't completely understand. As intelligences, we did not yet possess the identity and blessings that would come to us as their children. President Marion G. Romney said, "In origin, man is a son of God. The spirits of men 'are begotten sons and

---

19. Patrick Kearon, "He is Risen with Healing in His Wings: We Can Be More Than Conquerors," *Liahona*, May 2022, 38–39; emphasis added.

20. Gerrit W. Gong, "We Each Have a Story," *Liahona*, May 2022, 45.

daughters unto God' (D&C 76:24). Through that birth process, self-existing intelligence was organized into individual spirit beings."[21]

Intelligences could not and cannot make themselves into children of God. This gift of divine life as spirit children came freely and wholly by the grace of our heavenly parents. When we were born spiritually, they instantly conferred on us an eternal and sacred identity as their children. That identity is the foundational and most important part of who we are.

Our spiritual birth is a story of the love, power, and grace of God shedding itself forth abundantly, pouring down upon us insomuch that there was and is "not room enough to receive it" (Malachi 3:10). If we struggle to understand grace, reviewing our spiritual birth is a good place to start. This is because, perhaps next to the Atonement of Jesus Christ, the grace of God is nowhere so abundantly and instantly manifest as it is in our spirit birth—our divine origin.

Author Adam S. Miller wrote, "Grace, as the *original* enabling power, is manifest first and foremost in that original expression of God's divine power: creation itself."[22]

Why did our heavenly parents "have" us spiritually? How did they feel about us as "newborns"? Were they thrilled to receive a new spirit child into their family, similar to most parents on earth? Were we vulnerable and fragile like newborns in mortality? Did we look to our heavenly parents to meet our many needs? Did we cry out to them when we were upset, afraid or confused? Were they attentive to us? Did we love and adore them?

We don't know all of these answers completely, but we can confidently resolve many of these questions, even if by supposition. We know we were brought forth in tender love as the spiritual children of our heavenly parents. We know this because love is their central characteristic and eternal motivation. Certainly we were each wanted, celebrated, and cherished as their "newborn."

We were also surely vulnerable and fragile. We undoubtedly looked to them for help in every way and cried out to them in our

21. Marion G. Romney, "The Worth of Souls," *Ensign*, Nov. 1978, 14.

22. Adam S. Miller, *Original Grace* (Salt Lake City: Deseret Book, 2022), 81.

weakness, just as we often do now. And, just as now, our cries were answered with understanding, help, wisdom, and perfect love.

Yet *life* as their children was just the beginning of our divine identity. Along with life, they simultaneously gave us their perfect love, their perfect planning for our happiness and growth, their perfect Son, and their complete devotion.

God's matchless gift of life is always packaged together with His greatest gifts of love.

There was no randomness in our spirit birth. Our parents had created detailed plans (of salvation) for us before we "arrived" as their spirit children. They were undoubtedly united and prepared, through priesthood covenants, to help us become all and receive all.

From the time of our birth, they were wholly devoted to us, even to the point of suffering and sacrifice, as revealed in the appointment of our Savior and Redeemer, which required the greatest of all suffering in our behalf. "For God so loved the world, that he gave his only begotten Son, that whosoever believeth in him should not perish, but have everlasting life" (John 3:16).

Through God's grace, we also received agency at birth so we could choose their gifts and learn and grow. His gift of agency is also part of who we are. President David O. McKay said, "Next to the bestowal of life itself, the right to direct that life is God's greatest gift to man."[23]

Yet despite this generosity, love, planning, devotion, sacrifice, suffering, and gift of agency, sometimes we don't choose Him. We turn from Him, make mistakes, and even rebel in sin. We misuse our agency.

He knows we will make mistakes and sin. He knows everything. He is not surprised, angry, or disgusted with us. He has prepared the way for these failures to resolve as we return to Him through repentance. His mercy and patience are also part of our heritage and identity.

Just like agency is part of God's gift to us, repentance is also part of God's gift to us. He would not give us agency without repentance. Our heavenly parents did not have us so they could condemn us but so they could exalt us (see John 3:17).

---

23. *Teachings of Presidents of the Church: David O. McKay* (2003), 208.

Some faiths teach that we are not *children* of God but simply His *creations*. Certainly, to have identity as a creation of God is wonderful and great. But to be the offspring of heavenly parents is infinitely greater.

Jesus is clear on the point that we are God's children. He prayed, "*Our Father* which art in heaven, Hallowed be thy name" (Matthew 6:9-13; emphasis added). In the Doctrine and Covenants, Christ refers to God as "*your Father*, and your God" (Doctrine and Covenants 88:75; emphasis added). After Jesus was resurrected, He told Mary at the tomb, "Touch me not; for I am not yet ascended to my Father: but go to my brethren, and say unto them, *I ascend unto my Father, and your Father; and to my God, and your God*" (John 20:17; emphasis added).

Of our status as God's children, Elder Tad R. Callister said,

> There is a sentiment among many in the world that we are the spirit creations of God, just as a building is the creation of its architect or a painting the creation of its painter or an invention the creation of its inventor. The scriptures teach, however, a much different doctrine. They teach that we are more than creations of God; they teach that we are the literal spirit offspring or children of God our Father. What difference does this doctrinal distinction make? The difference is monumental in its consequence because *our identity determines in large measure our destiny*. For example, can a mere creation ever become like its creator? Can a building ever become an architect? A painting a painter? Or an invention an inventor? If not, then those who believe we are creations of God, rather than His spirit offspring, reach the inevitable conclusion that we do not have the capacity to become like our creator, God."[24]

Because we are God's children, with His potential, we are also given His work to do. We are invited to join the family business. As we do the work He gives us, He prepares us to receive our full inheritance as His children. As the Savior taught, "He that receiveth my Father receiveth my Father's kingdom; therefore all that my Father hath shall be given unto him" (Doctrine and Covenants 84:36-38).

---

24. Tad R. Callister, "Our Identity and Our Destiny," 1; emphasis added.

When we consider these elements of our divine identity (life, love, potential, agency, and work) all poured out upon us at birth, it is easier to understand why God often identifies us as children. The implications are infinite and include eternal life, eternal families, and eternal love. We can follow the pattern of our divine parentage precisely because we are children of heavenly parents. President Boyd K. Packer said, "Christ taught us to be 'perfect, even as your Father which is in heaven is perfect' (Matt. 5:48), to take on His attributes, to follow the pattern of our parentage."[25]

In God's way, *this* is what it means to be children, and especially to be *His* children. To be a child in His way means the greatest status and identity.

And that means *all* of us.

We are, in our very essence, the spirit children of God. There are other important aspects of our identity, but this central identity comes first.

---

25. Boyd K. Packer, "The Pattern of Our Parentage," 67.

3

I Am a Beloved Child of Heavenly Parents

"All human beings—male and female—are created in the image of God. Each is a beloved spirit son or daughter of heavenly parents, and, as such, each has a divine nature and destiny."[26]

If we struggle to remember our divine identity when we are being attacked and categorized by the adversary, let's remember that "all of [us] are children of the most High" (Psalms 82:6). Paul taught, "The Spirit itself beareth witness with our spirit, that we are the children of God" (Romans 8:16).

Our godly parentage is royal in the highest sense. President Boyd K. Packer taught, "Spiritually you are of noble birth, the offspring of the King of Heaven. Fix that truth in your mind and hold to it. However many generations in your mortal ancestry, no matter what race or people you represent, the pedigree of your spirit can be written on a single line. You are a child of God! Once we understand that

26. "The Family: A Proclamation to the World," ChurchofJesusChrist.org.

doctrine, that realization changes us. After that we cannot willingly hurt another. We then can yield to his discipline and accept even the very hard lessons of life."[27]

Ironically, for many of us, this highly flattering truth is not easy to accept or believe, let alone remember, day after day. Maybe this is because the truth is so complimentary. It sometimes might sound over the top to us. Besides, when we are feeling inclined to wander and to "do our own thing," we might actually want to forget these teachings. But whether these truths are known or unknown, cherished or neglected, remembered or forgotten, we are the children of heavenly parents.

When Moses is called to be a prophet, the Lord clearly wants Moses to understand his true identity as God's child. God appears to Moses "face to face" and says, "Behold, I am the Lord God Almighty, and Endless is my name; for I am without beginning of days or end of years; and is not this endless? And, behold, *thou art my son*; wherefore look, and I will show thee the workmanship of mine hands; but not all, for my works are without end, and also my words, for they never cease. . . . And I have a work for thee, *Moses, my son*" (Moses 1:3–4, 6; emphasis added).

God first needs Moses to understand *Him* as "the Lord God Almighty, and Endless is my name." Only then does Moses's true identity have full meaning as God's child. The Prophet Joseph Smith said, "If men do not comprehend the character of God, they do not comprehend themselves."[28]

After addressing Moses by name, God tenderly calls him "my son." God repeats this endearing way of speaking to Moses in the next verse: "Moses, my son." God calls upon Enoch using the same language: "Enoch, my son" (Moses 6:27). In our day, He calls on Joseph Smith in the First Vision, saying, "Joseph, my son, thy sins are forgiven thee."[29]

These are the expressions of a personal and affectionate parent who knows us. We come from "the Lord God Almighty," but He is

---

27. Boyd K. Packer, "To Young Women and Men," *Ensign*, May 1989, 54.

28. Joseph Smith, in *History of the Church*, 6:303–5.

29. "History, circa Summer 1832," 3, josephsmithpapers.org.

also an eternally kind and tender Father. As His children, we are the heirs of His perfect love and affection.

President Brigham Young said, "When you . . . see our Father, you will see a being with whom you have long been acquainted, and he will receive you into his arms, and you will be ready to fall into his embrace and kiss him."[30] With a similar tone, President Ezra Taft Benson taught, "Nothing is going to startle us more than when we pass through the veil to the other side than to realize how well we know our Father and how familiar His face is to us."[31]

Understanding our true identity helps us tenderly love each other and ourselves with greater patience and sensitivity, like our Father loves us. Elder Gifford Nielson said, "Our Heavenly Father wants us to love ourselves—not to become prideful or self-centered, but to see ourselves as He sees us: we are His cherished children."[32]

Heavenly Father even seems to reassure Jesus of His identity at His baptism. "And there came a voice from heaven, saying, Thou art my beloved Son, in whom I am well pleased" (Mark 1:11). Predictably, Satan soon tries to degrade Jesus's divine identity by using a deceptive phrase when tempting Him: "*If* thou be the Son of God" (Matthew 4:3, 6; emphasis added). At the end of Jesus's mortal ministry, Satan again attacks with these same words: "*If* thou be the Son of God, come down from the cross" (Matthew 27:40; emphasis added).

Jesus's identity was assailed by Satan literally from the beginning to the end of His ministry. We can surely expect similar assaults to be aimed at us.

How did understanding His divine relationship to God help Jesus through difficulties? How often did He affirm His identity to those around Him?

Jesus seems to have known His divine identity very early in life. As a boy, when He stays behind to teach in the temple, He reassures His worried mother by referring to His divine identity: "How is it that

---

30. Brigham Young, "Discourse," *Deseret News*, Oct. 1, 1856, 235.

31. Ezra Taft Benson, "Jesus Christ—Gifts and Expectations" (Brigham Young University devotional, Dec. 10, 1974), 8, speeches.byu.edu.

32. Gifford Nielson, "This is our Time!," *Liahona*, May 2021, 66.

ye sought me? wist ye not that I must be about my Father's business?" (Luke 2:49).

When we feel confused, naturally stating these eternal relationships can clarify for ourselves, and for those around us, exactly who we are—the children of God. During His mortal mission, Jesus frequently testified of His divine identity: "I am the light of the world: he that followeth me shall not walk in darkness, but shall have the light of life" (John 8:12). "The woman saith unto him, I know that Messias cometh, which is called Christ: when he is come, he will tell us all things. Jesus saith unto her, I that speak unto thee am he" (John 4:25–26). He identifies Himself by name to the Pharisees: "Verily, verily, I say unto you, Before Abraham was, I am" (John 8:58). He identifies himself personally to Thomas and those with him: "Jesus saith unto him, I am the way, the truth, and the life: no man cometh unto the Father, but by me" (John 14:6).

A few more verses into Moses's story, we likewise find Satan attacking his identity. Possibly Moses's newfound clarity is exactly why Satan acts. He does not want us to have, even briefly, a clear understanding of our true identity. Satan appears in person to Moses and says, "Moses, son of man, worship me" (Moses 1:12).

Is it true that Moses is a son of man? Yes, that's true. But it's also true, and far more important, that Moses is a son of God. This truth, which God emphatically and repeatedly just taught Moses, is exactly what Satan wants Moses and all of us to confuse and forget. If we believe we are descended only from man, or even from lower life forms, we will be more inclined to identify and to worship in worldly ways.

But Moses is full of the Spirit and knows the truth. He has just learned important things about himself, about God, and about their relationship to each other. He is not going to let his true status be diluted.

He says, "Who art thou? For behold, I am a son of God, in the similitude of his Only Begotten; and where is thy glory, that I should worship thee? . . . I can judge between thee and God; for God said unto me: Worship God, for him only shalt thou serve. Get thee hence, Satan; deceive me not; for God said unto me: Thou art after the similitude of mine Only Begotten" (Moses 1:13–16).

Like Moses, our identity is also "in the similitude of [His] Only Begotten" in many ways. We are also God's children. We also have a sacred work to do. We are also beloved of our heavenly parents. We will also be resurrected. We also can receive His covenants and eternal life. Although we have a long distance to go, in some important respects, we are already like Him, in His similitude—a comforting and encouraging truth about our identity.

Moses knows who he is and uses this powerful knowledge to overcome Satan's attacks. In this way, both Moses and Jesus Christ give us a pattern to follow when dealing with temptation, worldly labels, and weaknesses. It is to remember—and perhaps even to state out loud—who we are.

Rebecca (Mark's daughter and Sarah's sister) seems to have intuitively known this as a little girl. When she was about seven years old, she made a friend—we'll call her Jane—who was offended by Rebecca's efforts to choose the right. Frustrated, Jane blurted out, "Just be bad once, Rebecca!" But Rebecca responded, "Jane, I can't." Jane asked, "Why?" Rebecca thought for a moment and then said, "Because I'm unique." This impressed Jane and ended the confrontation.

Implied in this wise, simple, and childlike statement was Rebecca's divine and eternal identity. Also implied was Jane's eternal identity as well because Jane is also a daughter of God. Both Jane and Rebecca are precious to God and unique in their individual personalities, sacred work, and pathways that lead back to Him.

God has given us many ways to remember that we are the beloved children of heavenly parents. By divine design, our physical bodies show us our true identity, created in their image. A physical body is part of God's perfection and therefore also part of our precious, eternal destiny. Identity and the physical body is discussed in chapter 6.

As children of God, His spiritual characteristics are also inherently within us. As we notice these godlike elements in ourselves, we can better see our true identity and destiny. Elder Parley P. Pratt wrote, "An intelligent being, in the image of God, possesses every organ, attribute, sense, sympathy, affection, of will, wisdom, love, power and gift, which is possessed by God himself. But these are possessed by man . . . in embryo, and are to be gradually developed. They resemble a bud, a germ, which gradually develops into bloom, and then, by progress, produces the mature fruit after its own kind."[33]

Of all God's attributes that remind us that we are His children, maybe the most essential is love. Understanding our relationship to God is incomplete without trying to understand how much we are loved by Him. President Thomas S. Monson said, "Your Heavenly Father loves you—each of you. That love never changes. It is not influenced by your appearance, by your possessions, or by the amount of money you have in your bank account. It is not changed by your talents and abilities. It is simply there. It is there for you when you are sad or happy, discouraged or hopeful. God's love is there for you whether or not you feel you deserve love. It is simply always there."[34]

He loves us more than we can comprehend. He loves us so much that He sacrifices and suffers for us. Out of love, He does all He can to bring us the greatest joy, peace, knowledge, and power for good.

Sister Susan H. Porter said:

> Brothers and sisters, do you know how completely God, our Heavenly Father, loves you? Have you felt His love deep in your soul? When you know and understand how completely you are loved as a child of God, it changes everything. It changes the way you feel about yourself when you make mistakes. It changes how you feel when difficult things happen. It changes your view of God's commandments. It changes your view of others and of your capacity to make a difference.[35]

Because of our identity, we have the design, the purpose, and the capacity to feel His love and to learn to love ourselves and others like He does. God's perfect love is part of who we are.

President Dieter F. Uchtdorf said the following:

> No matter where you live, no matter how humble your circumstances, how meager your employment, how limited your

33. Parley P. Pratt, *Key to the Science of Theology* (Salt Lake City: Deseret Book, 1978), 61.

34. Thomas S. Monson, "We Never Walk Alone," *Ensign* or *Liahona*, Nov. 2013, 123–24.

35. Susan H. Porter, "God's Love: The Most Joyous to the Soul," *Liahona*, Nov. 2021, 33.

> abilities, how ordinary your appearance, or how little your calling in the Church may appear to you, you are not invisible to your Heavenly Father. He loves you. . . .
>
> Brothers and sisters, the most powerful Being in the universe is the Father of your spirit. He knows you. He loves you with a perfect love.
>
> God sees you not only as a mortal being on a small planet who lives for a brief season—he sees you as his child. He sees you as the being you are capable and designed to become. He wants you to know that you matter to Him.
>
> May we ever believe, trust and align our lives so that we will understand our true eternal worth and potential.[36]

We are the beloved children of our loving, all-powerful heavenly parents. By exercising some faith, this is relatively easy for most of us to accept. It makes intuitive sense. Being children of God defines all mankind equally as brothers and sisters and is the foundational part of our identity.

Yet there is still much, much more to understand.

---

36. Dieter F. Uchtdorf, "You Matter to Him," *Ensign* or *Liahona*, Nov. 2011, 22.

4

My Premortal Experiences Add to My Divine Identity

Our birth is but a sleep and a forgetting:
The soul that rises with us, our life's Star,
Hath had elsewhere its setting,
And cometh from afar:
Not in entire forgetfulness,
And not in utter nakedness,
But trailing clouds of glory do we come
From God, who is our home.
—William Wordsworth[37]

Thanks to the love and grace of our heavenly parents, our premortal spirit birth gave us new and glorious identity. We instantly had identity we had not previously possessed: new life with spirit bodies, divine parental love, endless potential and inheritance, the power of agency

37. William Wordsworth, "Our birth is but a sleep and a forgetting," Poetry Nook, accessed Jan. 24, 2023, https://www.poetrynook.com/poem/our-birth-sleep-and-forgetting.

as God's children, and new sacred purpose and work. Although we can't remember our birth as spirit children, it must have been wonderful and even stunning to leap forward into such a favored status and identity. Amazingly, our subsequent premortal experiences further "added upon" (Abraham 3:26) our birth-given identity in important ways.

As newly born spirit children, we gradually started to comprehend our marvelous situation. We came to know and love our heavenly parents. We met other spirit children, our sisters and brothers, including the Firstborn, Jesus Christ, then called Jehovah. This new family identity was comforting and promising. We surely rejoiced that family relationships are designed to be eternal.

Like now, we each had unique strengths, weaknesses, abilities, and desires. Some were introverted, others outgoing and charismatic. Some were ambitious and others less so. We nurtured social skills and made friends with those we admired and liked. With such friends, we may have participated in long conversations and even had fun together.

The premortal world was likely more complicated and organized than we suppose, with both informal moments and more formal occasions. President Russell M. Nelson noted:

> President Orson Hyde (1805–78), President of the Quorum of the Twelve Apostles, said "we understood things better [in the premortal world] than we do in this lower world." He continued, surmising about promises we likely made there: "It is not impossible that we signed the articles thereof with our own hands, which articles may be retained in the archives above, to be presented to us when we rise from the dead, and be judged out of our own mouths, according to that which is written in the books."[38]

Agency as children of God was new to us. We certainly struggled with some choices. As we gained knowledge and experience, we naturally became more responsible, hoping to be trusted someday with additional roles. Like now, we faced decisions to be humble or proud, honest or dishonest, selfless or selfish, believing or doubting. Our

---

38. Russell M. Nelson, "Choices for Eternity" (worldwide devotional for young adults, May 15, 2022), broadcasts.ChurchofJesusChrist.org.

choices impacted opportunities, molded our character, and further developed our identity.

Learning was an important part of our premortal experience. We likely had teachers and maybe even classes and homework! President Joseph F. Smith wrote, "Even before they were born, they, with many others, received their first lessons in the world of spirits and were prepared to come forth in the due time of the Lord to labor in his vineyard for the salvation of the souls of men" (Doctrine and Covenants 138:55–56). Similar to now, we were probably counseled to "seek learning, even by study and also by faith" (Doctrine and Covenants 88:118). Also like now, the things we learned and believed became part of us. "If a person gains more knowledge and intelligence in this life through his diligence and obedience than another, he will have so much the advantage in the world to come" (Doctrine and Covenants 130:18–19).

Undoubtedly we were grateful to be the children of our magnificent heavenly parents with all of the inherent marvelous implications. We probably thought of the future and wondered what might happen. Would our fondest dreams come true?

Some of God's valiant children—maybe you—participated in important discussions regarding our future. During the Grand Council, God's chosen leaders discussed the opportunities and risks of mortality, the need for opposition, the Fall of man, and the ultimate objectives: immortality and eternal life. The hostility toward God's plan was possibly also addressed.

After careful planning and much preparatory work, the time came for Heavenly Father to present His plan to everyone. We gathered to Him and listened excitedly. Most of us loved what we heard.

Heavenly Father shared with everyone the need to appoint a Savior and Redeemer to come to earth and overcome physical and spiritual death. He would have to suffer for us beyond all measure. He would need to be sinless. Only the dear and beloved Jehovah qualified (see Revelation 5:1–9). We would be required to place our complete faith in Him.

Satan coveted God's glory, and using his self-centered plan, he hoped to exalt himself. He said, "Behold, here am I, send me, I will be thy son, and I will redeem all mankind, that one soul shall not be lost, and surely I will do it; wherefore give me thine honor" (Moses 4:1; see also Isaiah 14:13–14).

Lucifer wickedly schemed to control everyone by removing our sacred gift of agency (see Moses 4:3). He told half-truths and manipulated the facts. He was persuasive and charismatic. Many sided with him, doubting Jehovah and opposing God. Possibly some feared the hard work and real risks of mortality. Others likely followed Lucifer's example, seeking vainglory of their own.

"But, behold, my Beloved Son, which was my Beloved and Chosen from the beginning, said unto me—Father, thy will be done, and the glory be thine forever" (Moses 4:2).

Then we were left to decide our individual course forward. Whom would we choose? Our choices for or against Jehovah would have a great impact on our future, our identity, and who we could become.

An epic battle for souls ensued. Certainly there were intense, trying moments. We saw some of God's beloved children, maybe our friends, fall into Lucifer's traps of deception, pressure, and charm. But we stood bravely, exercised compassion, testified of truth, and faithfully prayed for help.

It was the combined power of the Atonement of Jesus Christ and our testimonies in Him that eventually won this war of eternal consequence. John records:

> And there was war in heaven: Michael [Adam] and his angels fought against the dragon; and the dragon fought and his angels,
>
> And prevailed not; neither was their place found any more in heaven.
>
> And the great dragon was cast out, that old serpent, called the Devil, and Satan, which deceiveth the whole world: he was cast out into the earth, and his angels were cast out with him.
>
> And I heard a loud voice saying in heaven, Now is come salvation, and strength, and the kingdom of our God, and the power of his Christ: for the accuser of our brethren is cast down, which accused them before our God day and night.
>
> *And they overcame him by the blood of the Lamb, and by the word of their testimony.* (Revelation 12:7–11; emphasis added)

We meekly and bravely bore witness and thereby played an important role in winning that grand victory! Every time we bear our testimonies now, vocally or by example, we are again effectively overcoming Lucifer, but this time here on earth.

With enthusiasm, we chose Jehovah and even shouted for joy. Sister Barbara W. Winder said:

> How long has it been since you shouted for joy? In the Grand Council in heaven in our premortal existence, all the sons and daughters of God "shouted for joy" (Job 38:7). Our Father in Heaven gave us the opportunity to be born, to assume the responsibilities of mortality, which offered the opportunity of a "fulness of joy" (Ps. 16:11) but which also entailed risks of disobedience, sin, and heartache. Yet, as our Father's plan unfolded and we became aware of our divine potential for future immortality, we did all shout for joy.[39]

With Jehovah appointed by Heavenly Father and chosen by us, the plan moved forward. As Abraham 3:24–26 records:

> We will go down, for there is space there, and we will take of these materials, and we will make an earth whereon these may dwell;
>
> And we will prove them herewith, to see if they will do all things whatsoever the Lord their God shall command them;
>
> And they who keep their first estate [premortal life] shall be added upon; and they who keep not their first estate shall not have glory in the same kingdom with those who keep their first estate; and they who keep their second estate [earth life] shall have glory added upon their heads for ever and ever.

Our physical birth proves our prior decision to follow Jehovah. Elder Richard G. Scott said, "Every child of God in mortality chose the Savior's plan."[40] Therefore, we are born into mortality as known disciples of Jesus Christ. This designation as disciples of Jehovah was a powerful addition to our premortal identity. It is still a vital element of our identity now. If faithful, we will be identified as His disciples forever.

This premortal past of choosing the right, common to all of mankind, proves humankind's shared history of righteousness. That's

---

39. Barbara W. Winder, "Finding Joy in Life," *Ensign*, Nov. 1987, 95.

40. Richard G. Scott, "I Have Given You an Example," *Ensign* or *Liahona*, May 2014, 34.

helpful to remember when the adversary is telling us that we are bad in one way or another, something he regularly tries to do.

After our bravery and determination to follow Jehovah was established, He chose us to do His work on earth as His ministers. Battle-proven in the premortal world, we were given important missions and specific callings to carry out here. Through these assignments to serve Him, we obtained even further identity that we would take with us to earth as His ministers. In premortality, our identity was thus "added upon" in many important ways (see Abraham 3:26).

The Prophet Joseph Smith once said, "Every man [and woman] who has a calling to minister to the inhabitants of the world was ordained to that very purpose in the Grand Council of heaven before this world was. I suppose I was ordained to this very office in that Grand Council."[41]

This teaching is also found in the Book of Mormon: "And this is the manner after which they were ordained—being called and prepared from the foundation of the world according to the foreknowledge of God, on account of their exceeding faith and good works; in the first place being left to choose good or evil; therefore they having chosen good, and exercising exceedingly great faith, are called with a holy calling" (Alma 13:3).

Because we sustained Jehovah, we chose agency, or freedom, and rejected Lucifer along with his plan to deprive us of liberty. Part of our inborn divine identity, therefore, is as freedom fighters. The desire for liberty still burns brightly in the hearts of God's children on earth. The premortal battle continues here, and our role on earth remains much the same: to keep choosing agency, sustaining Jehovah through testimony, and rejecting Lucifer.

Because of our valiant role in the War in Heaven, the adversary knows us and despises us. We are correctly identified by him as his enemies because we were effective against him in the premortal world. Elder Robert D. Hales said, "We must remember that the adversary knows us extremely well. He knows where, when, and how to tempt

---

41. Joseph Smith, in *History of the Church,* 6:364.

us. If we are obedient to the promptings of the Holy Ghost, we can learn to recognize the adversary's enticements."[42]

Because of who we are, Lucifer still wants to control and destroy us. He is happy when we are hurt or have a bad day, but this is not his ultimate goal. He wickedly seeks our complete loss of agency, our loss of divine identity and destiny, our spiritual annihilation, our thorough destruction, and our total misery, death, and failure. He is the ultimate evil, the true enemy of our souls, body, and spirit (see 2 Nephi 4:27–28). His darkness, depravity, and maliciousness are unimaginable. This is who he is and what we are up against. Understanding identity means knowing we are on Lord's side. It also means knowing that Satan is on the opposing team.

Elder Richard G. Scott said, "Satan is no match for the Savior. Satan's fate is decided. He knows he has lost, but he wants to take as many with him as he can. He will try to ruin your goodness and abilities by exploiting your weaknesses. Stay on the Lord's side, and you will win every time."[43]

Sadly, Satan has already had significant success. In the premortal world, those who followed Lucifer lost much of their amazing birthright and identity. How many of our spiritual siblings followed Lucifer? The scriptures record, "And his tail drew the third part of the stars of heaven, and did cast them to the earth" (Revelation 12:4).

A third of the hosts of heaven cut themselves off from their infinite potential, turned their agency over to Lucifer, and turned their backs on the love, planning, suffering, and sacrifice of our heavenly parents and of Jehovah. Unhappily, these third of God's children lost who they were born to be. Their identity was not "added upon" but instead, because of their choices, was "subtracted from."

We face the same danger here on earth. Understanding our premortal experiences can give us perspective and strength.

Part of our mortal challenge is discovering our preordained work and then doing it. Wendy W. Nelson, the wife of President Russell M. Nelson, said, "The only thing that really matters is that you and

---

42. Robert D. Hales, "Becoming Provident Providers Temporally and Spiritually," *Ensign* or *Liahona*, May 2009, 7.

43. Richard G. Scott, "For Peace at Home," *Ensign* or *Liahona*, May 2013, 29–30.

I are doing exactly what we committed—even covenanted— in our premortal existence with our Heavenly Father we would do while we are here on earth. . . . My dear friends, in premortality you and I were each given wonderful missions to fulfill while we are here on earth. We have opportunities to fulfill our mortal missions, but we don't have to. No one will make us."[44]

Our premortal history is a big part of who we are. It is important for us to remember that before we were born, we were courageous warriors in choosing to follow Jehovah. Knowing this, we find reassurance that we can again succeed on earth—and continue following Him forevermore.

44. Wendy W. Nelson, "Hope of Israel" (worldwide youth devotional, June 3, 2018), supplement to the *New Era* and *Ensign*, ChurchofJesusChrist.org.

5

I Am a Beloved Child of God's Covenant

I remember, I remember,
The house where I was born,
The little window where the sun
Came peeping in at morn.
—Thomas Hood[45]

Our identity begins with our origins. Though this might sound obvious, birth is at the center of our origins, and it is therefore the center of our identity.

As discussed previously, prophets often teach of divine identity as tied to our status as children. Our divine identity as children most significantly began with our birth as spirit children to our heavenly parents in the premortal world. From that newly given and glorious position, our identity was further added upon in the premortal world

45. Thomas Hood, "I Remember, I Remember," Poetry Out Loud, accessed Jan. 24, 2023, https://www.poetryoutloud.org/poem/i-remember-i-remember/.

as we chose to support Heavenly Father's plan of salvation for us, put our faith in Jehovah, and stand valiantly against the adversary.

Therefore, the pattern of obtaining divine identity seems to be set forth in the premortal world: divine identity is granted through a divinely-appointed birth that endows us with godlike potential, love, gifts, heritage, purpose, and many privileges. Our identity is then added upon or diminished through our individual choices to reject or accept our birthright.

From God, we receive divine identity beyond our merit and understanding. This is also part of the pattern of obtaining divine identity. If we simply trust God, the ultimate origin of our existence, He abundantly pours out identity, love, and grace upon us, insomuch that there is "not room enough to receive it" (Malachi 3:10). All divine identity comes through His power and plans.

Following our spirit birth and subsequent premortal experiences, the next important step in the development of our divine identity would be to repeat this pattern, beginning with another divinely-appointed birth. And that's exactly what Heavenly Father proposed. We were offered more divine identity by being born again—this time physically.

The idea of a physical birth would surely have been exciting, if not overwhelmingly wonderful to us. We already knew that our perfect heavenly parents have physical bodies, and we rejoiced in the possibilities that physical birth would extend to us.

We must have wondered when this birth would take place. To whom would we be born? What new aspects of identity would be given? Would all of God's children receive this new birth?

The answer to the last question is no. Some—those who followed Lucifer—would choose not to be born physically. God accepts His children's decisions, even if those decisions mean their rejection of Him. He does not violate the agency He gave to us.

Doesn't this premortal offer of a new birth sound familiar to our experience now? Here on earth we face the same questions again. Will we, in mortality, choose our Heavenly Father's plan, place our faith in the Son of God, and be born again through His grace? We will discuss these mortal decisions and opportunities later.

Returning to the premortal world, this new birth—a physical birth—would also include a guaranteed physical *rebirth*, or resurrection. Through this birth and rebirth, we would be added upon in significant ways. In the premortal existence, all of God's children had adequate opportunity to accept this new offer from God.

When born into physical bodies on earth, we would gain a new status as children—"children of the covenant"—with additional divine identity, inheritance, purpose, and work to do. In the premortal world, we were *all* children of heavenly parents. Likewise, *everyone* born on earth is numbered among the "children of the covenant."

One of the most comforting parts of our identity as children of God is that we all have this status equally. There is no difference between us based on gender, race, age, disability, culture, socioeconomic status, or anything else. We are all the children of our heavenly parents, and through that identity, we each have the same love, blessings, potential, inheritance, purpose, and work.

The Book of Mormon states, "And he inviteth them all to come unto him and partake of his goodness; and he denieth none that come unto him, black and white, bond and free, male and female; and he remembereth the heathen; and *all are alike unto God*, both Jew and Gentile" (2 Ne. 26:33; emphasis added).

Just as we are equally children of heavenly parents, we are also equally the children of Adam and Eve. Before Adam and Eve began the family of mankind, they were sealed in marriage by priesthood covenant in the Garden of Eden. In 1835 when Joseph Smith began performing marriages, he declared that marriage was "an institution of heaven, instituted in the Garden of Eden."[46] Because Adam and Eve made this sealing covenant with God, their posterity became their covenant family and their covenant responsibility, designed and intended by God to be eternal. Adam and Eve's posterity became the new covenant family of God on earth through them.

Elder Orson Pratt taught, "Those who have received the ordinances of marriage according to the divine appointment are married for all eternity; [and] their children are the legal heirs to the inheritances, and glories, and powers, and keys and Priesthood of their fathers,

---

46. Joseph Smith, in *History of the Church*, 2:320.

throughout the eternal generations that are to come."[47] Through Adam and Eve's marriage covenant, this is our birthright as their children.

Just like there are many definitions of "Gentile," there are many definitions of "children of the covenant." Here, the definition applies that we are all the children of Adam and Eve and are therefore inheritors of their covenant promises. The phrase "children of the covenant" has other important meanings, including those who descend from Abraham, Isaac, and Jacob, or those who make the baptismal and temple covenants themselves.

Sometimes we might interpret the Abrahamic covenant as something that excludes part of humanity from identity as children of the covenant. We might believe that if we are not Abraham's direct descendants, or if we come from nonbelievers, then we are not actually of the covenant. We might think, "Maybe I can join the covenant, but I am not born with the covenant birthright."

This is not true. By virtue of our decision to be born physically into mortality, we are born equally as children of the covenant of Adam and Eve. Interestingly, it is Abraham's story that explains this so clearly.

Although Abraham's father did not follow the covenant path and was even led away into idolatry (see Abraham 2:5), Abraham nonetheless inherited through his father and father's fathers back to Adam his rightful place as a child of the covenant. Like everyone else, Abraham needed to accept and claim his birthright, but his status was there from birth, even though he was born to an unbelieving, wayward father.

Likewise, we inherit the rights to the priesthood through our righteous covenant ancestry, despite bad choices of our nearer ancestors, sometimes including our own parents (see Doctrine and Covenants: 86:8–10). Just like Abraham, we are also children of the covenant because we are the children of Adam and Eve. Furthermore, we are often the children of others who later made these covenants themselves, like Abraham and Sarah and even closer ancestors.

In the *Ensign*, Institute instructor S. Michael Wilcox explained, "Although we generally speak of the Abrahamic covenant beginning

---

47. Orson Pratt, in *Journal of Discourses*, 17:189.

with Abraham, he was actually the inheritor of promises, *passed down through the lineage of his fathers, that began with Adam.* Abraham himself wrote: 'And, finding there was greater happiness and peace and rest for me, I sought for the blessings of the fathers, and the right whereunto I should be ordained to administer the same; having been myself a follower of righteousness' (Abraham 1:2). Abraham desired and 'sought' the priesthood with all its accompanying promises. These blessings *'came down from the fathers, from the beginning of time'* (Abraham 1:3)."[48]

So, rest assured—there is no spiritual favoritism or inequality between us from birth. God gives divine identity to us equally when we are born in heaven spiritually and when we are born on earth physically. However, the choice is always ours whether to accept and claim our divinely given birthright.

This perspective does not detract from but rather adds to the importance of the Abrahamic covenant. We learn through Abraham and the covenant he made that we are all partakers of the original covenant promises, despite the choices and traditions of our nearer ancestors. That knowledge and assurance is part of the heritage of Abraham. He set the example before us in pursuing and claiming his covenant birthright through the covenant marriage of Adam and Eve.

The Lord reestablished His everlasting covenant through Abraham, Isaac, and Jacob. In this way, the Lord defined a new covenant family, patterned after Adam and Eve, to minister to the unbelieving world and help everyone accept and claim their birthrights as children of the covenant.

Understanding our covenant identity and birthright takes faith. President Russell M. Nelson said, "When we realize that we are children of the covenant, we know who we are and what God expects of us."[49] What does He expect of us? He expects us to make our own covenants with Him, to do our best to keep those covenants, and to bring His covenants to His children who do not have them.

---

48. S. Michael Wilcox, "The Abrahamic Covenant," *Ensign*, Jan. 1998; emphasis added.

49. Russell M. Nelson, "Covenants," *Ensign* or *Liahona*, Nov. 2011, 88.

When we accept and claim our birthright by making covenants of our own, we become children of the covenant in a new, formalized way. We join the Abrahamic covenant family of Jesus Christ and accept His covenant work. We are therefore born as children of the covenant, but we gain additional divine identity by accepting and claiming our birthright as we make these covenants ourselves. The phrase "children of the covenant" also often refers to this important meaning: those who make the covenants of God.

Our physical birth is patterned after our spiritual birth in the premortal world. Our spirit birth to our heavenly parents was not random. Likewise, our physical birth into mortality is not random, accidental, haphazard, or an afterthought. It is according to the perfect order, authority, grace, and plans of God for His faithful children. We are given physical birth and the accompanying status as children of the covenant because God, through His Son, meticulously planned for it, lovingly prepared for it, and graciously offered it to us. And we each chose His plan.

God prepared the world specifically for the physical births and mortal lives of His faithful children. Even if we were born on earth into challenging, depraved conditions, or to abusive or neglectful parents, our physical birth on earth is still a sacred, pivotal event. Physical birth is a necessary and monumental step for each of us in our eternal progression (see Appendix A).

Just because your physical birth came thousands of years after God's earlier preparatory, creative events, your "latter-day" arrival on earth is still sacred, still part of God's creative design, and still according to His divine direction and care. The placement of His children on earth at the beginning of time is no more planned, important, or precious to Him than your physical birth in the latter days at the end of time.

As children of heavenly parents, and as Adam and Eve's offspring, we are here by covenant, not by accident.

President Nelson said, "If the Lord were to speak to you, He would urge you to understand your identity—to know who you really are. He did so when He spoke to the people of ancient America. After identifying Himself, He informed His listeners of their identity."[50]

Let's pause and think about this. If you didn't know the content of the scripture President Nelson is about to quote, what would you guess the Lord says to the people about their identity? Maybe He would tell us we are God's children or that we are the beloved object of His work and glory, those for whom He suffered and sacrificed in indescribable ways. He could have said all of that to help us understand our identity, but He emphasized something else.

Continuing with the quote: "'Behold' he said, '*ye are* the children of the prophets; and *ye are* of the house of Israel; and *ye are* of the covenant which the Father made with your fathers, saying unto Abraham: And in thy seed shall all the kindreds of the earth be blessed' (3 Ne. 20:25; emphasis added). You share that same identity."[51] The next verse in Nephi reads, "And this because ye are the children of the covenant" (3 Nephi 20:26; emphasis added).

In this quote, we see both President Nelson and the Lord focusing on a sometimes overlooked part of divine identity. They emphasize that we are identified by our covenant relationship to His ancient prophets and to His ancient people. We are identified by the covenants of God (see also Mormon 7:1–2).

Here again we clearly see that our identity is often associated by prophets through our status as children. We are children of heavenly parents, we are children of the covenant, and we are children of Christ.

How exactly is our identity added upon as children of the covenant? How does our decision to be born on earth impact who we are? There are many glorious ways.

First, through our physical birth, we receive physical bodies and a subsequent resurrection after we die. A physical body is a huge leap forward in becoming more like our heavenly parents, and it is central to our divine identity. All who are born into the world will be resurrected after death, receiving a glorified, immortal physical body like they have.

---

50. Russell M. Nelson, "Identity, Priority, and Blessings," *Ensign*, Aug. 2001, 7.

51. Russell M. Nelson, "Identity, Priority, and Blessings," 7.

As children of the covenant, we receive many other amazing gifts. One gift is the birthright to be taught the gospel. We are equally loved and have an equal and generous chance to receive our Savior and inherit His greatest gift, eternal life (see Doctrine and Covenants 14:7).

Billions of God's children born on earth never learn about their favored status and rights as children of the covenant. Nevertheless, everyone will have such an opportunity, in either mortality or in the next world, through ministering and through vicarious temple work. No child of the covenant will be overlooked, as we are taught repeatedly through the Restoration.

Elder David B. Haight said, "One of the most profound principles of God's love for his children was revealed to Joseph Smith in the Kirtland Temple in 1836. In a vision he saw someone who had not received an opportunity to accept the gospel while living. A voice declared that all who have died without an opportunity to hear the gospel and accept it while on this earth will have the privilege in the spirit world."[52]

As children of the covenant, we also inherit endless love and devotion from our righteous ancestors, much like the love we inherited from our heavenly parents when we were born to them premortally. By divine design, we are meant to be an integral and eternal part of our covenant family on earth—a family that loves us and even needs us.

An important part of understanding the phrase "children of the covenant" is that we are the children of righteous, covenant ancestors. We belong to them and they to us. Understanding identity means understanding our covenant origins.

As children of the covenant, we intuitively sense this. Our ancestors, their lives, and their love are important to who we are, and the Light of Christ tells us we belong to each other and are meant to be an eternal family. According to prophecy, people worldwide are seeking out their ancestry. "Behold, I will send you Elijah the prophet before the coming of the great and dreadful day of the Lord. And he shall turn the heart of the fathers to the children, and the heart of the children to their fathers" (Malachi 4:5–6).

52. David B. Haight, "Joseph Smith the Prophet," *Ensign*, Nov. 1979, 24.

President M. Russell Ballard said:

> Knowing that we are loved by our Heavenly Father will help us know who we are and know that we belong to His great eternal family.
>
> The Mayo Clinic recently noted: "Having a sense of belonging is so important. . . . Nearly every aspect of our lives is organized around belonging to something." This report adds, "We cannot separate the importance of a sense of belonging from our physical and mental health"—and, I would add, our spiritual health. . . .
>
> Never forget that you are a child of God, our Eternal Father, now and forever. He loves you, and the Church wants and needs you. Yes, we need you![53]

Even beyond being loved, Elder Ballard shows how covenant belonging gives us identity through being needed. We belong *and* are needed in our families, including needed by those who have passed on (see Malachi 4:5–6). It's more than just belonging—we are key players, each and every one. This "being needed" is also part of our covenant identity.[54] We are born needy, but as children of the covenant, we are also born needed.

Being needed is a great blessing. Joseph Smith wrote, "And now, my dearly beloved brethren and sisters, let me assure you that these are principles in relation to the dead and the living that cannot be lightly passed over, as pertaining to our salvation. For their salvation is necessary and essential to our salvation, as Paul says concerning the fathers—*that they without us cannot be made perfect—neither can we without our dead be made perfect*" (Doctrine and Covenants 128:15; emphasis added).

All of this speaks to the strongest forms of love and belonging for each of us born on earth. Despite these truths, we might feel we don't belong or are not needed in the Church, even as baptized members. And sometimes we might believe we don't belong or are not needed

---

53. M. Russell Ballard, "Hope in Christ," *Liahona*, May 2021, 53.

54. Paul illustrated this concept by an analogy to our physical bodies (see 1 Corinthians 12:12–27). He wrote that just as all the parts of a body rely on each other and are necessary, so also we are needed as members of the covenant body of Christ, including our families and the Church.

in our families, even when we are sealed to them through temple covenants. But these feelings and ideas are from the adversary. The Savior and his prophets teach otherwise (see 1 Corinthians 12:12–31).

We *do* belong, and we *are* needed. We have a sacred work to do in the Church and in our families. It might take counseling together, study, and prayer to see how, but the eternal truth is clear—we belong and are needed in the Church and in our families whether we recognize it or not. That's who we are as children of the covenant.

When we are feeling down, worthless, vulnerable, or forgotten, if we can remember who we really are, then we will remember that we are basically good, have chosen righteously in the premortal world, and also that we belong and we are needed as members of our eternal families on earth and in heaven.

As children of the covenant, we receive other glorious promises and blessings. We are remembered and gathered if we stray, even generations later. "I will remember the covenant which I have made with my people; and I have covenanted with them that I would gather them together in mine own due time" (3 Nephi 20:29).

We see this taking place in the latter-day gathering of the children of Israel. We witness the beautiful blossoming and gathering of the children of Lehi. Part of the birthright of those drowned in the great flood was to be taught the gospel and gathered, even though they were destroyed for wickedness (see 1 Peter 3:18–20). The Lord does not forget His covenants, or His covenant children, even after they die. Gathering is happening on both sides of the veil.

Children of the covenant are therefore identified, remembered, and gathered by virtue of the covenants their parents made generations before they were born. This is another key way His covenants identify and define us.

Part of our heritage as children of the covenant is the blessing of the Light of Christ. John wrote that Jesus Christ is "the true Light, which lighteth every man [and woman] that cometh into the world" (John 1:9). President Boyd K. Packer said:

> Most members of the Church have a basic understanding of the Holy Ghost. Most have experienced its promptings and understand why the Holy Ghost is called the Comforter. They know "the Holy Ghost . . . is a personage of Spirit" (D&C 130:22) and a member of

> the Godhead (see A of F 1:1). But many do not know that there is another Spirit—"the light of Christ" (D&C 88:7)—another source of inspiration, *which each of us possesses in common with all other members of the human family.*[55]

All of these blessings are ours because we are the children of the covenant: physical birth, resurrection and immortality, the Light of Christ, belonging to the covenant family of Adam and Eve (which includes belonging and being remembered, loved, needed, and gathered), the guarantee of being taught the fulness of the gospel and ample opportunity to receive it completely, the right to seek and obtain all priesthood covenants, and our eternal destiny of eternal life. These unique blessings were not given to those who decided against physical birth.

We are children of heavenly parents. That glorious identity was added upon in the premortal world when we chose Jehovah and became His ministers. This growing and superlative identity was added upon further when we accepted God's plan and were born physically as children of the covenant.

Yet there is still so much more to our divine identity.

55. Boyd K. Packer, "The Light of Christ," *Ensign*, Apr. 2005, 8; emphasis added.

6

My Body Is Central to My Identity

"More amazing than raising the dead is that we live at all. A silent heart that beats again is not nearly as amazing as the heart that beats within your breast right now."
—Lawrence E. Corbridge[56]

Before moving forward, let's pause and discuss one key part of our identity as children of the covenant—our bodies.

Identity, at least partly, is defined by our very substance, our building blocks so to speak. Through the restored gospel, we know we were born as spirits first. "For I, the Lord God, created all things, of which I have spoken, spiritually, before they were naturally upon the face of the earth" (Moses 3:5). When we were born on earth, our physical bodies were added as temples for our spirits and also as temples for the Holy Ghost (see Doctrine and Covenants 121:34–35). Part of

56. Lawrence E. Corbridge, "Stand Forever" (Brigham Young University devotional, Jan. 22, 2019), 6, speeches.byu.edu.

our eternal identity and heritage includes these spiritual and physical building blocks.

President Russell M. Nelson wrote:

> The gift of our physical bodies is a transcendent miracle. A unique body is given to each of us by our loving Heavenly Father. He created it as a tabernacle for our spirits, to assist each of us in our quest to fulfill the full measure of our creation. Our bodies allow each of us to experience the great plan of salvation that He has designed for all His precious children. He wants us eventually to become more like Him and return to live with Him. That great blessing would not be possible without our first receiving a physical body in this probationary estate.[57]

We have physical bodies like our heavenly parents. In other words, by receiving these imperfect, fallible, and sometimes challenging physical bodies, we become more like our heavenly parents, not less. This is a doctrine almost unique to the Restoration. Elder James E. Talmage wrote, "It is peculiar to the theology of the Latter-day Saints that we regard the body as an essential part of the soul. . . . Nowhere, outside of the Church of Jesus Christ, is the solemn and eternal truth taught that the soul of man is the body and the spirit combined."[58]

From the very beginning of the Restoration, we find clear messaging by God the Father and His Son, Jesus Christ, that the physical body is sacred, important, and central to our eternal identity. Joseph Smith both saw and heard God the Father and Jesus Christ personally. Firsthand, he witnessed that They are separate beings with physical bodies and that we are created in Their image, literally. Lost "plain and precious" (1 Nephi 13:26) truths about the physical body and about identity were already being restored—as a first priority, it seems.

Twenty-three years later, in 1843, the Lord wanted to make sure these truths were not lost again. So, with only one year left in Joseph Smith's life, the Lord revealed to him these scriptural words to be recorded and kept: "The Father has a body of flesh and bones as tangible as man's; the Son also" (Doctrine and Covenants 130:22). Our

---

57. Russell M. Nelson, "Your Body: A Magnificent Gift to Cherish," *New Era*, Aug. 2019, 2.

58. James E. Talmage , in Conference Report, Oct. 1913, 117.

heavenly parents are perfect beings with perfect, physical bodies of flesh and bone.

We receive our basic physical characteristics and appearance from them. President Thomas S. Monson said, "God our Father has ears with which to hear our prayers. He has eyes with which to see our actions. He has a mouth with which to speak to us. He has a heart with which to feel compassion and love. He is real. He is living. We are his children, made in his image. We look like him, and he looks like us."[59]

With our mortal susceptibility to physical sickness, aging, and death, we know our spirits will be separated from our bodies at the end of our lives, according to God's plan. Nevertheless, we have assurance that after death, our spirits and bodies will be eternally united and made perfect like the bodies of our heavenly parents. "The soul shall be restored to the body, and the body to the soul; yea, and every limb and joint shall be restored to its body; yea, even a hair of the head shall not be lost; but all things shall be restored to their proper and perfect frame" (Alma 40:23).

Maybe we should take a moment and slow down this discussion. If we don't, we risk glossing over some astonishing points about who we are. Our creation as spirits with physical bodies might seem normal and even unremarkable, but these building blocks are truly miraculous.

Elder Lawrence E. Corbridge said:

> The most phenomenal occurrences of all time and eternity—the most amazing wonders, the most astounding, awesome developments—are the most common and widely recognized. They include: I am; you are; we are; and all that we perceive exists as well, from subatomic particles to the farthest reaches of the cosmos and everything in between, including all of the wonders of life. Is there anything greater than those ordinary realities? No. Nothing else even comes close. You can't begin to imagine, much less describe, anything greater than what already is.
>
> In light of what is, nothing else should surprise us. It should be easy to believe that with God all things are possible.

---

59. Thomas S. Monson, "I Know That My Redeemer Lives," in Conference Report, Apr. 1966, 63.

> The healing of the withered hand is not nearly as amazing as the existence of the hand in the first place. If it exists, it follows that it can certainly be fixed when it is broken. The greater event is not in its healing but in its creation.
>
> More phenomenal than resurrection is birth. The greater wonder is not that life, having once existed, could come again but that it ever exists at all.
>
> More amazing than raising the dead is that we live at all. A silent heart that beats again is not nearly as amazing as the heart that beats within your breast right now.[60]

We usually take our miraculous origins and existence (and therefore our identity) for granted. This lack of constant awe and appreciation is understandable. To be in an endless state of overwhelming amazement would be exhausting and impossible. Besides, we do not even remember life without our bodies. Nevertheless, we can strive to remember our bodies with reverence.

If you have trouble believing in miracles, maybe start with this: *you are a miracle*. Elder D. Todd Christofferson said:

> As God and Christ are deserving of our reverence, so their works are deserving of our respect and reverence. That of course includes the marvelous creation that is this earth. And yet as wonderful as this earth is, it is not the greatest of God's creations. Greater still is this marvelous physical body. It is in the very likeness of the person of God. It is essential to our earthly experience and key to our everlasting glory. . . . How are we to preserve the sanctity of this most important and sacred of God's creations? At a minimum, we would not in any way defile our bodies.[61]

The adversary knows our bodies are important to our identity and destiny. He and his evil followers have intelligence and spirits, but they do not and never will have physical bodies because they rejected Jehovah and the plan of God in the premortal world. Consequently, they are exceedingly jealous of our bodies, and out of hatred and

60. Lawrence E. Corbridge, "Stand Forever" (Brigham Young University devotional, Jan. 22, 2019), 6, speeches.byu.edu.

61. D. Todd Christofferson, "A Sense of the Sacred" (Brigham Young University devotional, Nov. 7, 2004), 3–4, speeches.byu.edu.

jealously, they try to make us feel bad about our physical bodies and misuse them.

The devil and his angels do everything they can to destroy our bodies and keep us from experiencing the joy that is inherent in uniting spirit with physical body. A fulness of joy only comes with the perfect unification of the spiritual and physical elements. "For man is spirit. The elements are eternal, and spirit and element, inseparably connected, receive a fulness of joy; And when separated, man cannot receive a fulness of joy" (Doctrine and Covenants 93:33–34).

The adversary and his followers attack us by whispering to us that we also should reject, hate, and even harm our bodies. If we listen, we might learn to hate part of our divine essence. By extrapolation, when we abuse or hate our bodies, we in part reject our own divine identity and the very identity of God.

Sometimes in mortality, in our recurrently confused and limited view of eternity, these demons can be convincing. We start to be ashamed of various aspects of or flaws within our amazing physical bodies. We might even learn to reject ourselves if we listen to the incessant and disparaging voices of the world.

Thankfully, the restored gospel of Jesus Christ gives us understanding of the physical body that provides clarity and empowers us against the demeaning lies of the adversary. Joseph Smith said, "We came to this earth that we might have a body and present it pure before God in the celestial kingdom. The great principle of happiness consists in having a body. The devil has no body, and herein is his punishment. He is pleased when he can obtain the tabernacle of man, and when cast out by the Savior he asked to go into the herd of swine, showing that he would prefer a swine's body to having none."[62]

This story in the New Testament clearly illustrates the jealousy of the devil and his angels toward our physical bodies:

> And when [Jesus] was come to the other side into the country of the Gergesenes, there met him two [people] possessed with devils, coming out of the tombs, exceeding fierce, so that no man might pass by that way.

---

62. *Teachings of the Prophet Joseph Smith*, sel. Joseph Fielding Smith (1976), 181.

> And, behold, they cried out, saying, What have we to do with thee, Jesus, thou Son of God? art thou come hither to torment us before the time?
>
> And there was a good way off from them an herd of many swine feeding.
>
> So the devils besought him, saying, If thou cast us out, suffer us to go away into the herd of swine.
>
> And he said unto them, Go. And when they were come out, they went into the herd of swine: and, behold, the whole herd of swine ran violently down a steep place into the sea, and perished in the waters.
>
> And they that kept them fled, and went their ways into the city, and told every thing, and what was befallen to the possessed of the devils (Matthew 8:28–33).

Perhaps Jesus allowed this dramatic destruction of the pigs to demonstrate that (1) the physical body is sacred and important, and (2) the devil, full of hatred, deception, and jealousy, does all he can to destroy any physical body at any time.

The Prophet Joseph Smith taught, "All beings who have bodies have power over those who have not. The devil has no power over us only as we permit him. The moment we revolt at anything which comes from God, the devil takes power."[63] Through our physical birth as children of the covenant, we therefore have power over the devil and his angels. Our bodies are a means of power in addition to a key to happiness. Power and joy through our physical bodies are part of our identity, now and forever.

Our imperfect physical bodies stand at the very center of our mortal test. Through these tests we are meant to be stretched and to grow. Elder David A. Bednar said:

> We are the spirit sons and daughters of God and have inherited divine qualities from Him. The precise nature of the test of mortality, then, can be summarized in the following questions: Will my body rule over my spirit, or will my spirit rule over my body? Will I yield to the enticings of the natural man or to the eternal man? That, brothers and sisters, is the test. We are here on

---

63. *Teachings of the Prophet Joseph Smith*, 181.

> the earth to develop godlike qualities and to learn to bridle all of the passions of the flesh.[64]

This means that by divine design, we are living in challenging circumstances. Having a physical body is similar to other challenging circumstances we experience in this fallen world. We are surrounded by mortal conditions that can lead us into temptation.

President Nelson wrote:

> Satan knows the power of our appetites. So, he tempts us to eat things we should not eat, to drink things we should not drink, and to desecrate the most intimate expressions of love by employing them outside the bounds of marriage.
>
> *When we truly know our divine nature, we will want to control such appetites.* And we will focus our eyes on sights, our ears on sounds, and our minds on thoughts that are a credit to our physical creation as a temple of God. In daily prayer, we will gratefully acknowledge Him as our Creator and thank Him for the magnificence of our own physical temple. We will care for it and cherish it as our own personal gift from God.[65]

The adversary hopes to demean the physical body and, in the process, demean our eternal identity. If he can make our body seem less sacred, he can make our identity seem less sacred. If he can make our body seem unimportant or less valuable, he can make our eternal identity seem unimportant or less valuable.

The gifts that come through our body are divine, especially the power to have children of our own. Elder David A. Bednar said:

> The power of procreation is spiritually significant. Misuse of this power subverts the purposes of the Father's plan and of our mortal existence. Our Heavenly Father and His Beloved Son are creators and have entrusted each of us with a portion of their creative power. Specific guidelines for the proper use of the ability to create life are vital elements in the Father's plan. *How we feel about and use*

---

64. David A. Bednar, "Ye Are the Temple of God," *Ensign*, Sept. 2001.

65. Russell M. Nelson, "Your Body: A Magnificent Gift to Cherish," *New Era*, Aug. 2019, 2; emphasis added.

> *that supernal power will determine in large measure our happiness in mortality and our destiny in eternity. . . .*
>
> Because a physical body is so central to the Father's plan of happiness and our spiritual development, Lucifer seeks to frustrate our progression by tempting us to use our bodies improperly.[66]

This diabolical work is manifest all around us. We see it in the media's glorification of violence, promiscuity, and drug abuse. We also see it in social media and body image lies, some of which sadly result in eating disorders that can lead to hospitalization or even death.

The prophets teach us to treasure what we have and avoid unhealthy comparisons. Elder Jeffrey R. Holland said, "We are all different. Some are tall, and some are short. Some are round, and some are thin. And almost everyone at some time or other wants to be something they are not! . . . We should all be as fit as we can be—that's good Word of Wisdom doctrine. That means eating right and exercising and helping our bodies function at their optimum strength. We could probably all do better in that regard. But I speak here of optimum health; there is no universal optimum size."[67]

All of the adversary's wicked efforts to demean our bodies simultaneously demean our identity. The more the adversary persuades us to see our bodies as unimportant or even as evil, the more confused we are about our identity in general because the very opposite is true. Our bodies are sacred, not evil; they are a conduit to progress, not an enemy or a barrier to progress.

President Russell M. Nelson said, "With your body being such a vital part of God's eternal plan, it is little wonder that the Apostle Paul described it as a 'temple of God.' Each time you look in the mirror, see your body as your temple. That truth—refreshed gratefully each day—can positively influence your decisions about how you will care for your body and how you will use it."[68]

---

66. David A. Bednar, "We Believe in Being Chaste," *Ensign* or *Liahona*, May 2013, 42; emphasis added.

67. Jeffrey R. Holland, "To Young Women," *Ensign* or *Liahona*, Nov. 2005, 29.

68. Russell M. Nelson, "Decisions for Eternity," *Ensign* or *Liahona*, Nov. 2013, 107.

The adversary tempts us to compare our bodies with others, which encourages envy, anxiety, depression, self-loathing, vanity, and pride. He also encourages us to misuse our bodies and to view them outside of their sacred purpose.

Sister Susan W. Tanner said, "Happiness comes from accepting the bodies we have been given as divine gifts and enhancing our natural attributes, not from remaking our bodies after the image of the world. The Lord wants us to be made over—but in His image, not in the image of the world, by receiving His image in our countenances (see Alma 5:14, 19)."[69]

Our physical bodies can help us understand and remember our divine identity and destiny. Little children are so thrilled with their new bodies. They want to run, jump, squeal, laugh, roll, and experience all the joy of uniting a body with a spirit. As children of the covenant, celebrating our precious physical bodies as temples of God is an act of gratitude and faith and an important part of understanding our divine identity and destiny.

---

69. Susan W. Tanner, "The Sanctity of the Body," *Ensign* or *Liahona*, Nov. 2005, 14–15.

7

Priesthood Covenants Add to My Divine Identity

"The time is always right to do what is right."
—Martin Luther King, Jr.[70]

When a baby girl is born to a queen and king, she is a princess. Yet after she is born, she can choose to accept her royal place or walk away from her birthright. She must choose her rightful status as a princess if she is to become what she was born to be—a queen.

In one way or another, this is often the pattern of classic literature and epic movies. Someone is born to greatness but shirks or doesn't realize their true identity. It takes time for them to comprehend the meaning of their birthright. Then, bravely, they begin to realize and accept their true destiny, claim and assume their lofty position, fully engage, and become what they were born to be, usually saving themselves and those around them from an almost overwhelming evil power.

70. Martin Luther King, Jr., "The time is always right," Reflect and Respond, accessed Jan. 25, 2023, https://reflectandrespond.com/the-time-is-always-right/.

This is the common story found in *Star Wars*, *Harry Potter*, *The Lord of the Rings*, *The Lion King*, *The Chronicles of Narnia*, and so forth. Why is this simple narrative so frequently the basis of the most popular literature and movies? Maybe it's because these concepts resonate with us personally.

As children of the covenant, this is our story too. We see it in the scriptures also, for example in Abraham, Joseph of Egypt, Moses, and Esther. This is the very intimate story of all the children of God.

We are each a princess or prince, born to the King and Queen of all. In the premortal world, our identity was added upon through our acceptance of our divine birthright. The same situation applies in mortality. One by one, we must discover, accept, and claim our true birthright identity as princesses and princes, heirs of the heavenly monarchs.

Elder Adeyinka A. Ojediran said, "Dear brothers and sisters, each of us is a prince or princess. We have been sent to mortality by a loving Heavenly Father to enjoy the blessing of a body that would become immortal through the Atonement and Resurrection of Jesus Christ. . . . Accepting the Savior's invitation means partaking of His ordinances and keeping our covenants with Him."[71]

God has already given us life, planned for us, sacrificed for us, accepted us, loved us, believed in us, and chosen us. He has granted to us our birthright. Covenants are about *our* choosing Him, believing in Him, loving him, accepting Him, obeying Him, and sacrificing for Him. No one else can accept our birthright for us.

***

Mark: Once when speaking to the young women and their parents at a fireside, I read a scripture which states, "I am Jesus Christ, the Son of God, who was crucified for the sins of the world, even as many as will believe on my name, *that they may become the sons [and daughters] of God*" (Doctrine and Covenants 35:2; emphasis added). After the meeting, I was approached by a concerned mother who told

71. Adeyinka A. Ojediran, "The Covenant Path: The Way to Eternal Life," *Liahona*, May 2022, 104–5.

me that the young women are *already* His daughters and that I had made it sound as if they were not.

We reread the above scripture together, but she was still not satisfied. "Are we the children of God or not?" she asked me in frustration.

"Yes, of course," I replied, feeling a bit confused.

This interaction prompted me to study further.

As I researched, I noticed that the scriptures teach that we are the children of God, but they also state we can *become* the children of God. By virtue of our physical birth, we are the children of the covenant, but prophets teach that we can also *become* the children of the covenant. We are all of Christ, those for whom He sacrificed and suffered, but we are also told in the scriptures how to *become* His children.

These might appear to be contradictions, but after a closer look, I slowly began to understand that they are not.

***

We are all born as God's precious children in each of these ways, just like a prince or princess is born. But that is not the end of it. Through God's covenants, we are invited to formally accept and claim our birthright status and thus *newly become* children of God, of the covenant, and of Christ. This process is much like royal children accepting and claiming their royal birth. President Russell M. Nelson said, "Children of the covenant have the right to receive His doctrine and to know the plan of salvation. They claim it by making covenants of sacred significance."[72]

Like the children of earthly royalty, as children of the King of Kings we also must choose what we will do with our birthright. We can walk away from it, or we can choose to accept and embrace it. Unsurprisingly, the Lord requires that we accept and claim our birthright in His way—the covenant way. We cannot accept and claim our divine birthright on our own terms.

In fact, this is exactly what Lucifer proposed. He wanted to claim his birthright in his own way, not God's. His plan, he said, was to save all the children of God. He aspired to become like God. Those

72. Russell M. Nelson, "Covenants," *Ensign* or *Liahona*, Nov. 2011, 88.

proposals deceptively sound like righteous desires, consistent with his divine birthright. But Lucifer was in rebellion, scheming to remove agency and take forceful control of everyone. For that deception and defiance, he and his followers were cast out and denied their precious birthrights.

Inspired by Lucifer, this same pattern repeated itself at the Tower of Babel. They said they wanted to build a temple in their own way. They wanted God to come to it. They said they desired to get to heaven through this building. Those seem to be righteous desires. But they were in full revolt, rejecting God's ways. They proudly had their own plans and ideas for doing things. For that pride and willful rebellion, their languages were confused and they were scattered.

This was also true of Cain. He claimed he wanted to worship God and to sacrifice to Him. But Cain did not want to do it in God's way. Was Cain really trying to sacrifice obediently to God? No, he was deceiving himself with pride, and his true intentions were revealed as he killed his brother for personal gain, using secret combinations with the devil.

If we look carefully, we sometimes see this disturbing pattern in ourselves. We might proudly want to get closer to God in *our* way but not His—maybe through nature, but not through prayer, scriptures, the Church, covenants, or complete repentance. We'll keep the commandments mostly, we might say, except for [fill in the blank]. We'll believe in ancient prophets, but not all the modern ones. We'll accept callings, but please, not *that* calling.

Priesthood ordinances and covenants are God's required way. The Heavenly King offers us covenants to claim our royal birthright as His offspring.

When we make covenants and are baptized, ordained, washed, anointed, endowed, and sealed, our birthright moves from being unaccepted and unclaimed to authoritatively accepted and claimed. Making covenants with God changes us from weak to empowered, from uncommitted to formally committed, from unendowed to endowed, from unsealed to sealed and bound to Him in His way. Elder D. Todd Christofferson said, "The covenants God offers to His children do more than guide us. They bind us to Him, and, bound to Him, we can overcome all things."[73]

God's covenants formalize our status as children of Christ. "And now, because of the covenant which ye have made ye shall be called the children of Christ, his sons, and his daughters; for behold, this day he hath spiritually begotten you" (Mosiah 5:7).[74]

Through God's covenants, we also formalize our status as children of the covenant. President Nelson said, "In *every* age, the temple has underscored the precious truth that those who make covenants with God and keep them are children of the covenant."[75] Making and keeping His covenants formally binds us to our families on earth and to our ancestors and posterity forever. As President Nelson also taught, "We all have our agency. We can choose to be of Israel, or not. We can choose to let God prevail in our lives, or not."[76]

Covenants likewise formalize our identity as children of our heavenly parents. "But as many as received him, to them gave he power to become the sons [and daughters] of God, even to them that believe on his name" (John 1:12).

The covenants therefore formally add to our identity in familiar ways: as children of God, of the covenant, and of Jesus Christ. Covenants also "add upon" our divine identity in many new ways. For example, when we make the covenant of baptism and confirmation, we can receive the gift of the Holy Ghost, which President Wilford Woodruff called "the greatest gift we can receive in mortality."[77]

This gift exemplifies how the covenant path moves us toward our divine destiny. The Holy Ghost teaches, guides, refines, and sanctifies

---

73. D. Todd Christofferson, "Why the Covenant Path," *Liahona*, May 2021, 118.

74. Russell M. Nelson said, "When we embrace the gospel and are baptized, we are born again and take upon ourselves the sacred name of Jesus Christ. We are adopted as his sons and daughters and are known as brothers and sisters. He is the Father of our new life. We become joint heirs to promises given by the Lord to Abraham, Isaac, Jacob, and their posterity" ("Children of the Covenant," *Ensign*, May 1995, 34).

75. Russell M. Nelson, "The Temple and Your Spiritual Foundation," *Liahona*, Nov. 2021, 94.

76. Russell M. Nelson, "Let God Prevail," *Liahona*, Nov. 2021, 92.

77. *The Discourses of Wilford Woodruff*, ed. G. Homer Durham (1990), 5.

us, helping us become who we are designed to be. The temple endowment (gift) of spiritual power and priesthood authority is a further example of receiving, here and now, covenant inheritance and associated divine help. These covenant gifts add upon our identity.

Covenants are the means God utilizes to turn our divine identity into divine destiny. Elder D. Todd Christofferson asked, "What, then, is the difference of the covenant path? Actually, the difference is uniquely and eternally significant. It includes the nature of our obedience, the character of God's commitment to us, the divine help we receive, the blessings tied to gathering as a covenant people, *and most importantly, our eternal inheritance.*"[78]

Regarding our eternal inheritance, the covenants of the Lord that build on each other from baptism to the sacrament to marriage in the temple can be viewed as divine estate planning with signatures on pages of documents—covenants made over time and in sequence, with Christ as our cosigner. President Nelson said, "The doctrine of Christ helps us find and stay on the covenant path. Staying on that narrow but well-defined path will ultimately qualify us to receive all that God has. Nothing could be worth more than all our Father has!"[79]

Our greatest destiny can only come to us through His highest covenant, the covenant of eternal marriage. "In the celestial glory there are three heavens or degrees; And in order to obtain the highest, a man [and woman] must enter into this order of the priesthood [meaning the new and everlasting covenant of marriage]; And if he [or she] does not, he [or she] cannot obtain it" (Doctrine and Covenants 131:1–3).

Ultimately, when we are sealed in the temple to our spouse, we are authorized by God to become parents in His way, as eternal families. We become more and more like them as we also plan for and bring forth a covenant family, love our offspring unconditionally, teach them the gospel, set an example, and suffer and sacrifice for our children, giving all we can so that they might have their complete, eternal inheritance.

---

78. D. Todd Christofferson, "Why the Covenant Path," 117; emphasis added.

79. Russell M. Nelson, "Pure Truth, Pure Doctrine, and Pure Revelation," *Liahona*, Nov. 2021, 6.

We thus transition from identity through our status as children to identity through our status both as children *and* as parents. Significantly, as covenant mothers and fathers, we participate in the godlike work of helping grant identity to our children. Elder Tad R. Callister said, "Participation in the saving ordinances unlocks and unleashes certain powers of godliness in our lives that are not available in any other way. These powers help refine us and perfect us."[80]

God's covenants also strengthen our divine identity through higher-level commitments. Elder D. Todd Christofferson said, "With covenants, we are intent on more than just avoiding mistakes or being prudent in our decisions. We feel accountable to God for our choices and our lives. We take upon us the name of Christ. We are focused on Christ—on being valiant in the testimony of Jesus and on developing the character of Christ. With covenants, obedience to gospel principles becomes rooted in our very soul."[81]

Understanding and accepting our true identity is a challenging and lifelong process for all of us. It requires the daily work of renewing meekness, faith, and repentance. As we try, bumbling along as we are prone to do, we sometimes wander into forbidden paths, experiment with things outside of God's intentions and design, and consequently fail to find our divine purpose and true meaning. Hopefully we are like the prodigal son who eventually "came to himself" (Luke 17:15) and returned to his father and to his true identity.

That the prodigal son "came to himself" seems especially meaningful in the discussion of divine identity. Even though he was born as his parents' son, he turned away from his birthright. Even though he had a privileged standing, he squandered his inheritance and tried to redefine "himself."

But through repentance, he was already redeemable as "himself," his parents' son. Through repentance, he could access "himself," an

---

80. Tad R. Callister, "Our Identity and Our Destiny" (Brigham Young University devotional, Aug. 14, 2012), 8, speeches.byu.edu.

81. D. Todd Christofferson, "Why the Covenant Path," 117. The Old Testament teaches something similar: "This shall be the covenant that I will make with the house of Israel; After those days, saith the Lord, I will put my law in their inward parts, and write it in their hearts; and will be their God, and they shall be my people" (Jeremiah 31:31, 33).

heir. He, "himself," still had a family and a place simply by accepting and claiming his birthright. His divine identity, or "himself," was still available.

He decided to repent and return home, and "when he was yet a great way off, his father saw him, and had compassion, and ran, and fell on his neck, and kissed him [and] said to his servants, Bring forth the best robe, and put it on him; and put a ring on his hand, and shoes on his feet" (Luke 15:20, 22).

When his son returned, repented, and accepted his birthright, his father seems to have formalized the family relationship with a robe, a ring, and shoes—all emblems used in sacred covenants. Having chosen his rightful place, the son began to realize his divine identity and to pursue his divine destiny. His birthright identity was now being "added upon."

In addition to all of this, God's covenants give us something very comforting—powerful assurance of who we are. When we meekly and formally choose Him by covenant, we are enabled by Him to see our divine identity more clearly. God's covenants give us convincing evidence that He knows us by name, accepts us individually, and believes in and loves us perfectly.

"Therefore, in the ordinances thereof, the power of godliness is manifest" (Doctrine and Covenants 84:20).

8

Work Is Central to My Divine Identity

Two roads diverged in a wood, and I—
I took the one less traveled by,
And that has made all the difference.
—Robert Frost[82]

When a princess chooses her birthright role, she is shown her destiny in greater detail. She is given rules to keep and work to do. She enters into a time of training and preparation. She is not yet ready to be queen.

When we choose our royal birthright through covenants, we are shown our divine destiny in greater detail. We are given rules to keep and work to do, entering into something analogous to an apprenticeship. We are told this training will take time. "There was a space granted unto man in which he might repent; therefore this life became

82. Robert Frost, "The Road Not Taken," Poetry Foundation, accessed Jan. 24, 2023, https://www.poetryfoundation.org/poems/44272/the-road-not-taken.

a probationary state; a time to prepare to meet God; a time to prepare for that endless state which has been spoken of by us" (Alma 12:24).

Our divine identity points us toward our work, and our work points us toward our divine destiny. Decisions regarding our work determine our destiny. President Thomas S. Monson said, "I can't stress too strongly that decisions determine destiny. You can't make eternal decisions without eternal consequences."[83]

When we accept our birthright, we covenant to learn all we can while we faithfully work and practice. Practice is a good word because it implies we are learning and making mistakes in this phase. By seeing ourselves and each other as apprentices in training, maybe we will have more patience with ourselves and others when we make mistakes, which we all do.

What exactly is our covenant work or apprenticeship? In the most basic terms, keeping God's commandments is our work, as the scriptures teach. "Behold, this is your work, to keep my commandments, yea, with all your might, mind and strength" (Doctrine and Covenants 11:20).

When we claim our birthright by covenant, we learn more of our sacred apprenticeship work within the ordinances themselves. For example, in the sacramental prayer, it says that those who partake of the sacrament "witness unto thee, O God, the Eternal Father, that they are willing to take upon them the name of thy Son, and always remember him and keep his commandments which he has given them" (Doctrine and Covenants 20:77).

Our apprenticeship work as princesses and princes is designed to move us toward our royal destiny. As we improve at keeping the commandments, we literally become more like God, who keeps all the commandments perfectly. "If thou wilt enter into life, keep the commandments" (Matthew 19:17).

We also covenant to love one another, and as we improve in love, we become more like God, who loves everyone perfectly. We covenant to serve one another, and as we learn to serve each other better, we become more like Jesus Christ, who serves perfectly. Within the most

83. Thomas S. Monson, "Decisions Determine Destiny" (Brigham Young University devotional, Nov. 6, 2005), 3, speeches.byu.edu.

sacred covenants, we are given the sacred and demanding work of building an eternal family because eternal family is the very center of Their work. Covenant work moves us from accepting and claiming our birthright toward actually becoming what we are meant to become.

Therefore, repentance and the Atonement of Jesus Christ are at the core of our work. Repentance means becoming, little by little, all we are designed to be. Repentance is the central process of accepting, understanding, and realizing our divine identity. The degree to which we embrace Jesus Christ and His gift of daily repentance is the degree to which we will understand, remember, and realize our divine identity.

President Russell M. Nelson said, "Nothing is more liberating, more ennobling, or more crucial to our individual progression than is a regular, daily focus on repentance. Repentance is not an event; it is a process. It is the key to happiness and peace of mind. When coupled with faith, repentance opens our access to the power of the Atonement of Jesus Christ."[84]

Regarding our covenant work, Amulek taught, "For behold, this life is the time for men [and women] to prepare to meet God; yea, behold the day of this life is the day for men [and women] to perform their labors" (Alma 34:32–33).

We might learn more and more about our identity, and even have a strong spiritual witness of who we are, but this learning is little better than theory until we meekly engage in the work of faith and repentance and thus truly begin to understand and become who we are designed to be. "If any man will *do* his will, he shall *know* of the doctrine" (John 7:17; emphasis added).

President Nelson taught, "When we choose to repent, we choose to change! We allow the Savior to transform us into the best version of ourselves. We choose to grow spiritually and receive joy—the joy of redemption in Him. When we choose to repent, we choose to become

---

84. Russell M. Nelson, "We Can Do Better and Be Better," *Ensign* or *Liahona*, May 2019, 67.

more like Jesus Christ!"[85] Because we are children of God, our divine destiny is to become more like Jesus Christ.

Our work of keeping the commandments could also be described as our stewardship as disciples of the Lord Jesus Christ. As His disciples, His work becomes our work. Mormon emphasized this part of divine identity by saying, "Behold, I am a disciple of Jesus Christ, the Son of God. I have been called of him to declare his word among his people, that they might have everlasting life" (3 Nephi 5:13).

Mormon identified himself by his work of discipleship. "Behold, I am a disciple of Jesus Christ" is a profound and powerful statement of divine identity tied to covenant work.

Like Mormon, discipleship is part of who we are. We chose Jehovah in the premortal world. As we accept His covenants on earth, we again formalize our discipleship. If we ever feel tempted, compromised, vulnerable, or confused, we can gain strength and clarity like Mormon as we remind ourselves, "I am a disciple of the Lord Jesus Christ. That is who I was before I was born on earth, who I am now, and who I will be forever."

Our work of keeping the commandments could also be defined as the work of gathering Israel, including ministering to the covenant people, doing missionary work, and performing temple and family history work. President Nelson said:

> There is nothing happening on this earth right now that is more important than [gathering Israel]. There is nothing of greater consequence. Absolutely nothing.
>
> This gathering should mean everything to you. This is the mission for which you were sent to earth. . . .
>
> Anytime you do anything that helps anyone—on either side of the veil—take a step toward making covenants with God and receiving their essential baptismal and temple ordinances, you are helping to gather Israel. It is as simple as that.[86]

The work of gathering Israel is the Lord's great latter-day work. As His children, it is ours also. Prophets have been very specific regarding

---

85. Russell M. Nelson, "We Can Do Better," 67.

86. Russell M. Nelson, "Hope of Israel" (worldwide youth devotional, June 3, 2018), supplement to the *New Era* and *Ensign*, ChurchofJesusChrist.org.

blessings for those involved in missionary work, family history, and temple work. Elder Richard G. Scott said, "Do you young people want a sure way to eliminate the influence of the adversary in your life? Immerse yourself in searching for your ancestors, prepare their names for the sacred vicarious ordinances available in the temple, and then go to the temple to stand as proxy for them to receive the ordinances of baptism and the gift of the Holy Ghost. As you grow older, you will be able to participate in receiving the other ordinances as well. I can think of no greater protection from the influence of the adversary in your life."[87] There are many other amazing family history and temple blessings that are related to understanding identity.[88]

Our work of keeping the commandments could also be described as the work of seeking charity, the pure love of Christ. Elder Dieter F. Uchtdorf said, "Christ knows how to minister to others perfectly. When the Savior stretches out His hands, those He touches are uplifted and become greater, stronger, and better people as a result. If we are His hands, should we not do the same? We can love as He does."[89]

As we learn to love as He loves, we become like Him. When we seek charity, we are pursuing the very center of His identity and our destiny. In the following quote, note the ways (marked in italics) that charity helps us become like Him:

"Wherefore, my beloved brethren, pray unto the Father with all the energy of heart, *that ye may be filled* with this love, which he hath bestowed upon all who are true followers of his Son, Jesus Christ; *that ye may become the sons of God*; that when he shall appear *we shall be like him*, for *we shall see him as he is*; that we may have this hope; *that we may be purified even as he is pure*. Amen" (Moroni 7:48 emphasis added).

Even though we all have the same work of keeping the commandments through repentance, discipleship, gathering Israel, and learning

---

87. Richard G. Scott, "The Joy of Redeeming the Dead," *Ensign* or *Liahona*, Nov. 2012, 94.

88. For a sample of such apostolic promises, see Dale G. Renlund, "Family History and Temple Work: Sealing and Healing," *Ensign* or *Liahona*, May 2019, 47.

89. Dieter F. Uchtdorf, "You Are My Hands," *Ensign* or *Liahona*, May 2021, 70.

to love, we each walk a distinctive path toward our divine destiny. As we learn and do our unique personal work, it will change us forever.

President Nelson taught how to find our sacred purpose and special work. He said:

> Learn for yourselves who you really are. Ask your Heavenly Father, in the name of Jesus Christ, how He feels about you and your mission here on earth. If you ask with real intent, over time the Spirit will whisper the life-changing truth to you. Record those impressions, review them often, and follow through with exactness.
>
> I promise you that when you begin to catch even a glimpse of how your Heavenly Father sees you and what He is counting on you to do for Him, your life will never be the same![90]

That is inspiring, practical, and very specific advice from a prophet of God. Pray, ask, be patient, listen for impressions, write them down when they come, review them, and carefully follow through. Repeat. Learn things that will change your life forever! When we recognize the work God has for us, and dedicate it as such, our divine identity becomes increasingly clear to us.

A friend of Sarah's once said that she knew her job as a nurse was consecrated by God because she had new opportunities to share the gospel with each assignment. She received spiritual assurance that nursing was part of her sacred purpose. The Lord teaches, "Verily I say, men should be anxiously engaged in a good cause, and do many things of their own free will, and bring to pass much righteousness; For the power is in them, wherein they are agents unto themselves. And inasmuch as men do good they shall in nowise lose their reward" (Doctrine and Covenants 58:27–28).

Often, our patriarchal blessings help us understand our unique work and identity. Sister Bonnie H. Cordon said, "At an FSY conference, I met two young women who had been struggling. Both young women mentioned turning to her patriarchal blessing to rediscover the Lord's love and guidance for her personally. Find your patriarchal blessing, blow off the dust if you must, but study it often. If you

---

90. Russell M. Nelson, "Stand as True Millennials," *Ensign*, Oct. 2016.

don't have one, get one—soon. Don't delay finding out what the Lord wants to tell you now about who you are."[91]

As we study our patriarchal blessings, follow President Nelson's counsel, and seek to receive personal revelation, our unique paths will emerge. Maybe God has an important way for you to use your ability in art, athletics, business, cooking, counseling, government, health care, landscape, law, leadership, management, music, marriage, parenting, research, teaching, science, or any number or combination of other things. Our pathways will be distinctive to us. As we study the lives of the leaders of the Church, we see important work guided by God in many walks of life. The covenants inherently tie our identity to our work and our work to our destiny.

We see this pattern in the life of Jesus Christ. His divine *identity* led to His divine work. His unique work resulted in His divine *destiny.* It has been said, "The Lord gets His work done through His people and gets His people done through His work" (anonymous).

Without Jesus Christ's identity as the Only Begotten Son of God, He would not have been given His unique work. Without doing His work of creating the universe, He would not be the Creator. Without the overarching work of the Atonement, He would not be our Savior and Redeemer. "For to this end Christ both died, and rose, and revived, that he might be Lord both of the dead and living" (Romans 14:9).

This concept of destiny through work is true for the adversary as well. His chosen purpose and work of rebellion, deception, and pride eventually defined him as the devil and resulted in his limited, miserable, and confused destiny. He had been endowed with divine identity, but he rejected God's plan for him and instead chose his own errant way. "How art thou fallen from heaven, O Lucifer, son of the morning! how art thou cut down to the ground, which didst weaken the nations!" (Isaiah 14:12).

Likewise, what we do with our divinely given identity will impact our destiny. If we are to obtain all the Father has to give us, if we are to become all we are designed and destined by Him to become, we

---

91. Bonnie H. Cordon, "Come unto Christ and Don't Come Alone," *Liahona*, Nov. 2021, 10.

must also, like the Savior, accept and claim our divine identity and learn and do the accompanying work.

Our divine identity is so full of hope and clarity. Yet this is not easy to accept or remember in mortality. In fact, as we try to understand our divine work, we might be compared to a young horse trying to get used to a saddle on its back.

When a saddle is first introduced to a horse, it is uncomfortable with the sensations and idea. It bucks and kicks. Eventually, most horses stop fighting and begin to tolerate the saddle and rider. Over the course of time, the horse typically matures in understanding, learns to accept the feel of the saddle, and is less anxious when a rider mounts. Eventually, the horse appreciates it's important role, becomes productive, loves the meaningful work, and relishes the feeling of doing what it is designed to do. Its identity as a horse translates into its work, and its work transforms it into becoming what it was meant to become.

Though quoted previously in the chapter about the premortal world, these words by Sister Wendy W. Nelson are also relevant here: "The only thing that really matters is that you and I are doing exactly what we committed—even covenanted—in our premortal existence with our Heavenly Father we would do while we are here on earth. . . . My dear friends, in our premortal existence you and I were each given wonderful missions to fulfill while we are here on earth. We have opportunities to fulfill our mortal missions, but we don't have to. No one will make us."[92]

Jesus Christ understands His apprentices perfectly. He suffered specifically so that He would know how to train us, teach us, help us, relate to us, and make sure we are never alone or misunderstood in our rigorous training. He came to earth to show us the way.

"And he will take upon him death, that he may loose the bands of death which bind his people; and he will take upon him their infirmities, that his bowels may be filled with mercy, according to the flesh,

---

92. Wendy W. Nelson, "Hope of Israel" (worldwide youth devotional, June 3, 2018), supplement to the *New Era* and *Ensign*, ChurchofJesusChrist.org.

that he may know according to the flesh how to succor his people according to their infirmities" (Alma 7:12).[93]

Even more than just understanding and teaching us perfectly, our Master and Teacher also loves us perfectly and is completely devoted to us, to the ultimate degree of suffering and sacrifice. We apprentices are in the best hands as we seek His help in our covenant work.

We access His mentorship through the means He provides: scriptures, prayer, priesthood covenants, prophetic counsel, and personal revelation. We also access His help through His other children. God often helps us through a friend, fellow covenant member, or Church leader.

As His disciples, ministering and mentoring in His name is part of our work too. God works through us, even though we are novices, to help our sisters and brothers in their apprenticeships. President Dieter F. Uchtdorf taught, "We are the hands of Christ. . . . As we emulate His perfect example, our hands can become His hands; our eyes, His eyes; our heart, His heart."[94]

93. See also Hebrews 2:18; Mosiah 4:16; 7:29; Doctrine and Covenants 62:1; 81:5.

94. Dieter R. Uchtdorf, "You Are My Hands," 68.

9

I Am a Beloved Child of Jesus Christ

"For unto us a child is born, unto us a son is given: and the government shall be upon his shoulder: and his name shall be called Wonderful, Counsellor, The mighty God, The everlasting Father, The Prince of Peace."
—Isaiah 9:6

We've reviewed our wonderful identity as children of heavenly parents and as children of the covenant. In many ways, our status as children of Christ is the capstone. He gloriously completes our identity and brings us to our divine destiny. We are His.

When we were born spiritually to our heavenly parents, we were brand new, so to speak—inexperienced, immature, and incomplete spiritually. We were subject to error, sin, and therefore spiritual death (defined as our separation from God). Despite our glorious *spiritual birth* as children of heavenly parents, we lacked completion. We needed (and need) *spiritual rebirth* through Christ to be clean and complete spiritually and restored to God's presence, overcoming spiritual death once and for all.

Likewise, when we were *physically born* to our earthly parents, we were imperfect and incomplete, subject to pain, disease, injury, and physical death. Despite our new glorious identity as children of the covenant, we lacked (and lack) completion physically. When we die, we will need *physical rebirth* through Christ to be restored to our resurrected physical body—whole, perfect, and immortal—if we are to overcome physical death, once and for all.

Both spiritually and physically, we therefore require new birth and new identity. In the Book of Mormon, Jacob wrote about these two rebirths through Christ:

> O how great the goodness of our God, who prepareth a way for our escape from the grasp of this awful monster; yea, that monster, death and hell, which I call the death of the body and also the death of the spirit.
>
> And because of the way of deliverance of our God, the Holy One of Israel, this death, of which I have spoken, which is the temporal [physical], shall deliver up its dead; which death is the grave.
>
> And this death of which I have spoken, which is the spiritual death, shall deliver up its dead; which spiritual death is hell; wherefore, death and hell must deliver up their dead, and hell must deliver up its captive spirits, and the grave must deliver up its captive bodies (2 Nephi 9: 10–12).

Our premortal spiritual birth to our heavenly parents was a specific, defined event, as was our mortal physical birth. Our resurrection, or physical rebirth, will also be a specific occasion. These births and rebirth provide us an instantaneous, glorious new identity each time.

Spiritual rebirth, on the other hand, is a process. However, there are many defined events along the way that help us to be reborn spiritually and gain identity anew through Jesus Christ. Two of these are repentance and making priesthood covenants. But ultimately, the process of spiritual rebirth culminates in a specific event: our exaltation—the ultimate, final, fully expressed rebirth through Jesus Christ. It is at the moment of our exaltation when our separation from God, caused by sin, is completely overcome and we are invited into the presence of our heavenly parents, never again to be separated. It is in exaltation that our identity is made complete and becomes our destiny.

Through the Atonement of Jesus Christ, we are "born again" (John 3:3), become "his seed" (Mosiah 15:11–12), and are "begotten" of Him (Doctrine and Covenants 76:24). Yet *all* of our births come through Jesus Christ, even our first birth spiritually to our heavenly parents. They would not have brought us forth as their spirit children without a Redeemer to overcome spiritual death. God would not have offered us a physical birth on earth without a Savior to overcome physical death.

Jesus Christ was prepared "from the foundation of the world" so that all of God's children might be born and then reborn physically and spiritually: "And behold, Enoch saw the day of the coming of the Son of Man, even in the flesh; and his soul rejoiced, saying: The Righteous is lifted up, and the Lamb is slain from the foundation of the world" (Moses 7:47; see also Revelation 13:8, Mosiah 4:7).

He earned the right to claim us as His own.

The Atonement of Jesus Christ for God's children had specific requirements. It would necessitate suffering and sacrifice in the greatest degree. It had to be performed by someone who was completely trustworthy, sinless, and able. The divine identity, potential, and destiny of all mankind rested on His shoulders alone from the very beginning.

Only He could meet all of the criteria. "There was no other good enough to pay the price of sin. He only could unlock the gate of heav'n and let us in."[95] The success or failure of God's plan to exalt His children began and ended with Jesus Christ. "I am Alpha and Omega, the beginning and the ending, saith the Lord, which is, and which was, and which is to come, the Almighty" (Revelation 1:8).

All of our covenants, births, and rebirths depend on Him. All of our new beginnings through repentance depend on Him. Ironically, the entire weight of the universe that He created rests on His shoulders. Elder Richard G. Scott said, "The Atonement is that essential ingredient of our Father in Heaven's plan of happiness without which that plan could not have been activated."[96]

---

95. "There Is a Green Hill Far Away," *Hymns,* no. 194.

96. Richard G. Scott, "He Lives! All Glory to His Name!," *Ensign* or *Liahona,* May 2010, 76.

Without Jesus Christ, we literally lose our spiritual and physical lives. It seems almost impossible to overstate His importance. "For if there be no Christ there be no God; and if there be no God we are not, for there could have been no creation. But there is a God, and he is Christ, and he cometh in the fulness of his own time" (2 Nephi 11:7). Through His Atonement, Jesus creates, saves, and redeems our divine identity and our divine destiny.

We are His.

We did not merit our spirit birth in the premortal world. We did not merit our physical birth on earth. Likewise, we cannot merit our resurrection (our physical rebirth). These births were superlative gifts from the infinite and incomprehensible generosity of God's grace through the Atonement of His Son, Jesus Christ.

Eternal life, the greatest of all the gifts of God (see Doctrine and Covenants 14:7), is likewise an essentially unearned, pure, and divine gift that comes to us through Jesus Christ's work of Atonement. We can reject it, turn it down, and walk away from God's loving invitations, but we cannot make exaltation happen on our own power or ability any more than we can make happen our resurrection, our physical birth, or our premortal spirit birth. President Dieter F. Uchtdorf said, "Even if we were to serve God with our whole souls, it is not enough, for we would still be 'unprofitable servants.' We cannot earn our way into heaven; the demands of justice stand as a barrier, which we are powerless to overcome on our own. But all is not lost. The grace of God is our great and everlasting hope."[97] As Paul wrote, "By grace are ye saved through faith; and that not of yourselves: it is the gift of God" (Ephesians 2:8–9).

What does it mean, through Jesus Christ, to realize our full identity as the children of heavenly parents? It means to become like Him, kings and queens to Him. In Revelation 1:5–6, it describes Jesus Christ as "the faithful witness, and the first begotten of the dead, and the prince of the kings of the earth . . . him that loved us, and washed us from our sins in his own blood, and *hath made us kings [and queens] and priests [and priestesses] unto God* and his Father; to him be glory and dominion for ever and ever" (emphasis added). Further,

---

97. Dieter F. Uchtdorf, "The Gift of Grace," *Ensign* or *Liahona*, May 2015.

Revelation 5:9–10 states, "Thou wast slain, and hast redeemed us to God by thy blood out of every kindred, and tongue, and people, and nation; And hast made us unto our God *kings [and queens] and priests [and priestesses]: and we shall reign on the earth*" (emphasis added).

As if to emphasize that these ancient blessings apply to both men and women, modern prophets bear witness specifically of women's divine destiny. President Joseph Fielding Smith wrote, "It is within the privilege of the sisters of this Church to receive exaltation in the kingdom of God and receive authority and power as queens and priestesses."[98]

Jesus gives us this opportunity. He also teaches us the lofty vision of our divine destiny. "What manner of men ought ye to be? Verily I say unto you, even as I am" (3 Nephi 27:27).

Through His loving Atonement, we do more than simply return to our Father in Heaven or to the innocence and glorious identity of our spiritual and physical births. His work is a work of completing us, of perfecting us, and of exalting us. He gives us new, perfected identity. Through Jesus Christ, we begin with divine but vulnerable *identity* and end with divine and everlasting *destiny.*

President Russell M. Nelson said to a group of young adults, "These truths ought to prompt your ultimate sense of FOMO—or fear of missing out. You have the potential to reach the celestial kingdom. The ultimate FOMO would be missing out on the celestial kingdom, settling for a lesser kingdom because here on earth you chose only to live the laws of a lesser kingdom."[99]

Even though we are born incomplete as spirit children to our heavenly parents, and born incomplete as physical children to our earthly parents, we are *reborn* complete and perfect physically and spiritually to Jesus Christ, the author and finisher of our identity and divine destiny.

Love is at the center of our identity and destiny. The love of Jesus Christ is the central aspect of His character and of His Atonement.

---

98. Joseph Fielding Smith, "Relief Society—an Aid to the Priesthood," *Relief Society Magazine*, Jan. 1959, 5–6.

99. Russell M. Nelson, "Choices for Eternity" (worldwide devotional for young adults, May 15, 2022), broadcasts.ChurchofJesusChrist.org.

He loves us in an infinite, perfect, and eternal way because of who He is. His courage comes from His love. "Perfect love casteth out fear" (1 John 4:18).

His love for us is so powerful that it is impossible for us to completely comprehend, especially if we are struggling to feel His love due to strong negative emotions or sin.[100] Nevertheless, His love, like the love of our heavenly parents, is the strongest validation of our identity. Jesus's love for us reflects our divine identity and His.

John the Apostle repeatedly referred to himself as the "disciple whom Jesus loved" (John 21:7). This self-designation by John identifies him in an important way. We can rightly take this comforting and encouraging title to ourselves as part of our identity. In fact, going back to the premortal world where we chose to follow Him, we have long been among His disciples whom He loves.

Elder Jeffrey R. Holland said, "However late you think you are, however many chances you think you have missed, however many mistakes you feel you have made or talents you think you don't have, or however far from home and family and God you feel you have traveled, I testify that you have not traveled beyond the reach of divine love. It is not possible for you to sink lower than the infinite light of Christ's Atonement shines."[101]

The adversary does not want us to know who we are, so he tries to prevent us from knowing about or feeling the love of the Savior. On the contrary, the adversary wants us to feel, incorrectly, that we are unimportant, not loved, and even forgotten. He hopes we feel unworthy of love. He knows that if we accept God's love and feel the pure and infinite love of Jesus Christ, we will desire to follow Him and to understand who we really are.

The adversary is very successful in his evil schemes to make us feel alone and unloved. He has many effective techniques and is relentless

---

100. "The influence of the Holy Ghost can be obscured 'by strong emotions, such as anger, hate, … [or] fear, … like trying to savor the delicate flavor of a grape while eating a jalapeño pepper. … [One flavor] completely overpowers the other'" (Dale G. Renlund, "Your Divine Nature and Eternal Destiny," *Liahona*, May 2022, 70).

101. Jeffrey R. Holland, "The Laborers in the Vineyard," *Ensign* or *Liahona*, May 2012, 33.

in his efforts. Sadly, we see this manifest in some forms of anxiety and depression, in suicide, in addiction, and in violence.

Despite all that, Jesus is determined to help us know who He is and who we are. He does this by always loving us and encouraging us to love each other. Isaiah described the infinite and unstoppable love of Jesus Christ like this: "Can a woman forget her sucking child, that she should not have compassion on the son of her womb? yea, they may forget, yet will I not forget thee. Behold, I have graven thee upon the palms of my hands; thy walls are continually before me" (Isaiah 49:15–16). We are so much defined by Him, and He by us, that we are "graven" upon the palms of His hands! Our walls (weakness, sin, challenges, and burdens) are *continually* before Him!

His love for us is proven through His life and especially His Atonement. He suffered for us as only He could. This suffering was personal, intimate, and complete. He understood and experienced everything difficult about our brokenness, sins, trials, difficulties, pain, fleeting joy, success, devastating failure, and weakness when He suffered for us.

Jesus Christ's divine suffering added perfect understanding to perfect love. Sister Chieko N. Okazaki wrote:

> It's our faith that He experienced everything—absolutely everything. Sometimes we don't think through the implications of that belief. We talk in great generalities about the sins of all humankind, about the suffering of the entire human family. But we don't experience pain in generalities. We experience it individually.
>
> That means He knows what it felt like when your mother died of cancer—how it was for your mother, how it still is for you. He knows what it felt like to lose the student body election. He knows that moment when the brakes locked and the car started to skid. He experienced the slave ship sailing from Ghana toward Virginia. He experienced the gas chambers at Dachau. He experienced Napalm in Vietnam. He knows about drug addiction and alcoholism.
>
> Let me go further. There is nothing you have experienced . . . that He does not also know and recognize. . . . He understands about rape and infertility and abortion. His last recorded words to his disciples were, "And, lo, I am with you always, even unto the end of the world." He understands your mother-pain when your

> five-year-old leaves for kindergarten, when a bully picks on your fifth-grader, when your daughter calls to say that the new baby has Down syndrome. He knows your mother-rage when a trusted babysitter sexually abuses your two-year-old, when someone gives your thirteen-year-old drugs, when someone seduces your seventeen-year-old. He knows the pain you live with when you come home to a quiet apartment where the only children are visitors, when you hear that your former husband and his new wife were sealed in the temple last week, when your fiftieth wedding anniversary rolls around and your husband has been dead for two years. He knows all that. He's been there. He's been lower than all that. He's not waiting for us to be perfect. Perfect people don't need a Savior. He came to save his people in their imperfections. He is the Lord of the living, and the living make mistakes. He's not embarrassed by us, angry at us, or shocked. He wants us in our brokenness, in our unhappiness, in our guilt and our grief.[102]

His Atonement shows us He understands and loves us, and it also shows He believes in us. His belief in us is part of our divine identity. He would not have immeasurably suffered for us if He did not believe in us because of who we are. He knows we can succeed on earth in the most important way—in His way. The adversary would have us believe we are worthless and cannot succeed in anything.

Based on Jesus's identity and ours, He asks us to love and to believe in Him, to love and to believe in ourselves, and to love and to believe in each other. This is difficult, especially if we are struggling to love and to believe in ourselves. Nevertheless, His endorsement is the strongest of validations of our identity. He is all-knowing, and He knows we can become what we are designed to become. His suffering is profound evidence that He approves us for His work.

His Atonement is complete, sealed up, and delivered. It is simply our job to receive His amazing love, endorsement, and gifts. His question to the Pharisees, "What think ye of Christ?" (Matt. 22:42), is therefore central in understanding our own identity. What do we think of Him? Do we know His true identity? Do we believe Him and receive Him? Do we feel His love for us?

---

102. Chieko N. Okazaki, *Lighten Up!* (Salt Lake City: Deseret Book, 1993), 174.

To make sure we know who He is, Jesus boldly clarifies His special position frequently and in a variety of ways. President Nelson said, "Jesus often established his own identity, then the identity of his followers."[103] We can be confident in who He is because He is confident in who He is. As we gain confidence in who He is, we will gain confidence in who we are too.

Jesus repeatedly clarifies His identity by stating His name and divine mission. To help us realize who He is, He openly does things only He can do. To further show us His identity, His disciples perform miracles in His name and by His power. These miracles include creating the world; turning water into wine; healing the crippled, blind, and critically ill; calming the raging sea; feeding the thousands; walking on water; raising the dead; teaching in His divine way; and appearing to the Nephites, to Joseph Smith, and to many others through time.

His greatest miracle is His Atonement. Ultimately and most importantly, Jesus teaches and testifies of His divine identity through His suffering, sacrifice, resurrection, and ascension into heaven.

Jesus boldly and clearly testifies and teaches of His true identity through parables, through prophesy, and through questions. He teaches of His divine identity through His miraculous birth and through His baptism, where Heavenly Father also testifies of Jesus's identity. "Jesus, when he was baptized, went up straightway out of the water: and, lo, the heavens were opened unto him, and he saw the Spirit of God descending like a dove, and lighting upon him: And lo a voice from heaven, saying, *This is my beloved Son, in whom I am well pleased*" (Matthew 3:16–17; emphasis added).

Jesus Christ continues to testify to the world of His divine identity through all of His creations, covenants, ordinances, commandments, the Book of Mormon, other scriptures of the Restoration, His modern-day prophets, His covenant members, His continued miracles in our lives, and His presence, gifts, and love. He also testifies of His identity through the Holy Ghost, for "the Comforter knoweth all things, and beareth record of the Father and of the Son" (Doctrine and Covenants 42:17).

---

103. Russell M. Nelson, "Children of the Covenant," *Ensign*, May 1995, 32.

Jesus said, "Though I bear record of myself, yet my record is true: for I know whence I came, and whither I go. . . . It is also written in your law, that the testimony of two men is true. I am one that bear witness of myself, and the Father that sent me beareth witness of me" (John 8:14–18).

We cannot understand our divine identity until we understand the identity of Jesus Christ. One day soon, His identity and our identity through Him will be clearly before us. President Nelson taught:

> In a coming day, you will present yourself before the Savior. You will be overwhelmed to the point of tears to be in His holy presence. You will struggle to find words to thank Him for paying for your sins, for forgiving you of any unkindness toward others, for healing you from the injuries and injustices of this life.
>
> You will thank Him for strengthening you to do the impossible, for turning your weaknesses into strengths, and for making it possible for you to live with Him and your family forever. His identity, His Atonement, and His attributes will become personal and real to you.[104]

Because of Him, we are alive, cherished, enabled, endorsed, endowed, gifted, heirs, loved, purchased, reborn, recommended, redeemed from sin, saved from death, sealed, succored, supported, trusted, and understood. Without the Atonement of Jesus Christ, we would be unclean and unforgiven, cut off from God forever. Jesus Christ preserves and enables our eternal identity as children of heavenly parents and as children of the covenant.

Elder Steven J. Lund said, "[We] cannot wait for the world to right itself before [we] come to know the Savior. Some are making decisions even now that they would not make if they understood their true identities—and His."[105]

---

104. Russell M. Nelson, "Study the Savior's Words," *New Era*, Jan. 2018.

105. Steven J. Lund, "Finding Joy in Christ," *Ensign* or *Liahona*, Nov. 2020, 37.

10

Understanding Divine Identity and Destiny

The destiny of man is in his own soul.
—Herodotus[106]

Learning to see ourselves as God sees us is the central challenge of understanding divine identity and destiny. In the Old Testament, the children of Israel said they saw themselves as grasshoppers and their enemies as giants (see Numbers 13:33). God saw them as His children, the children of His covenant, and the children of Christ. In response, the Lord said to Moses, "How long ere they believe me, for all the signs which I have shewed among them?" (Numbers 14:11).

Understanding divine identity is understanding reality.

Elder Joseph B. Wirthlin said, "We see ourselves in terms of yesterday and today. Our Heavenly Father sees us in terms of forever.

106. Herodotus, "The destiny of man," AllAuthor, accessed Jan. 23, 2023, https://allauthor.com/quotes/141141/.

Although we might settle for less, Heavenly Father won't, for He sees us as the glorious beings we are capable of becoming."[107]

As we see ourselves and others as our heavenly parents see us, life comes into a more profound perspective. Small things bother us less. The things of eternity matter more. We have increased courage, practice more patience with ourselves and others, and feel real purpose.

One might think that believing we are born as royalty with limitless potential would make us arrogant, but accepting divine identity is humbling. When we see our identity as God-given, we recognize our dependence. Our very lives are from Him. Our bodies, heartbeat, and breath are divine gifts. All the good we have—our families, potential, sacred work, divine identity, and destiny—come from and depend on Him. There is no room for arrogance in that understanding.

After all, we cannot create for ourselves anything close to our divine identity. We are already the children of all-knowing, all-loving, all-powerful heavenly parents. We can't improve on that origin.

Are there greater plans than their plans for us? No. Is someone more devoted to us than they are? No. Does someone offer us greater potential than the potential we have as their children? No. It's not even close.

It's humbling to submit to our divine birthright from our heavenly parents, to embark on their boat, to go with their flow, and to depend on this over our own judgment, inclinations, and worldly wisdom. Ironically, despite their wondrous and reassuring promises, accepting our divine identity is so humbling that it can feel quite difficult to choose.

Moreover, we are often correctly identified by worldly positions, many of which we might enjoy, even covet, and at least temporarily prefer. It's tempting to want to be called by titles such as teacher, counselor, technician, president, founder, professor, businesswoman, graduate, manager, leader, and so forth. Many of these designators are accurate and important in their individual ways. The difficulty is humbly and always acknowledging them as secondary.

---

107. Joseph B. Wirthlin, "The Great Commandment," *Ensign* or *Liahona*, Nov. 2007, 29–30.

Kevin Worthen, president of Brigham Young University, said, "Let us strive to view others first as children of God. Our initial inclination as fallen individuals is to view those in front of us primarily by their gender, race, political affiliation, sexual orientation, economic class, or other distinguishing features. Those identities can be important from time to time, but all of them are secondary all the time."[108]

Remembering that we are all first and foremost children of God helps us humbly see everyone as equals. We are equally born, equally loved by God, equally suffered for, equally His, and equally given the most important opportunities. As God's children, we are not designed to compete with each other—we are designed to cooperate with each other. Understanding identity helps us focus on our sacred work, which means we are better able to focus on others instead of ourselves.

Understanding and accepting divine identity is a great destroyer of pride and a powerful equalizer of humanity.

The perspective of divine identity brings many blessings in addition to humility and the recognition of equality. Understanding identity allows us to enthusiastically accept our sacred purposes and divine work instead of the purposes and work of the world. We also find real joy—joy that can only be found in the Lord's way. President Russell M. Nelson said, "If we look to the world and follow its formulas for happiness, we will never know joy. The unrighteous may experience any number of emotions and sensations, but they will never experience joy! Joy is a gift for the faithful. It is the gift that comes from intentionally trying to live a righteous life, as taught by Jesus Christ."[109]

When we accept our divine destiny, we leave behind the frenzied race of the world and find actual rest for our souls. The need to be richer than our neighbors is replaced with the desire to love them. We cease pining for fame and instead pine for more faith in the Savior. Hope in Christ replaces hope for more and more material goods. Lust and selfishness are dismissed by love and service. Meekness replaces posturing and pride.

---

108. Kevin J. Worthen, "Hearts Knit Together in Love" (Brigham Young University devotional, Sept. 7, 2021), 4, speeches.byu.edu.

109. Russell M. Nelson, "Joy and Spiritual Survival," *Ensign* or *Liahona*, Nov. 2016, 84.

Jesus said, "Come unto me, all ye that labour and are heavy laden, and I will give you rest. Take my yoke upon you, and learn of me; for I am meek and lowly in heart: and ye shall find rest unto your souls. For my yoke is easy, and my burden is light" (Matthew 11:28–30).

In history, we find inspiring stories among those who understood their divine identity. These stories often include miraculous forgiveness of others who have caused deep harm, such as prison guards in concentration camps, abusers, and drunk drivers who have taken lives.

Perhaps the ultimate example of such forgiveness is Jesus Christ on the cross. He knew the true identity of those who tortured Him, and He knew His own identity. He also knew that those Roman soldiers did not understand such things. So He prayed for them with love borne of understanding: "Father, forgive them, for they know not what they do" (Luke 23:34). Likewise, with understanding and love, He also suffered for us in our weakness and vulnerability, and He prays for our forgiveness too. Victor Frankl said, "Those who have a *why* to live for can bear with almost any *how*."[110]

It is only through Jesus Christ that we are truly and completely defined. When we surrender to Him all other identities, we humbly allow Him to define us. As we do so, He heals, simplifies, balances, magnifies the good, and helps us reject that which is incorrect. Because of our identity and His, He constantly labors with all His infinite love to help us find joy in the journey and eventually to become all we are meant to become, even designed to become, through Him.

Kim B. Clark, president of Brigham Young University–Idaho, said:

> If you seek to understand and live up to your eternal identity, it will grow in your mind and in your heart. When you face decisions or are tempted to do something that is wrong, when you face adversity and challenges, or when you are blessed with prosperity, the Holy Spirit will remind you who you are and will help you see your true identity and purpose with an eternal perspective. . . .
>
> A spiritual understanding and witness of your eternal identity and purpose will encourage you and give you hope. It will help you

---

110. Viktor E. Frankl, *Man's Search for Meaning* (New York: Simon and Schuster, 1985), 97.

> see the powerful connection between your identity and the Savior Jesus Christ. It will help you feel the never failing love of the Father and His Son and the blessings of light, power, and joy that your Father in Heaven has prepared for you."[111]

The Lord simplifies and clarifies who we are. After all is said and done, we are His. We are His beloved, His apprentices, His friends, His saved and redeemed. We are His disciples, His ministers, His heirs, His endowed, His chosen, His children, His covenant people. We are His work and His glory (see Moses 1:39). By the power of the Holy Ghost, as we understand and accept our true identity, we can each assuredly say, "I am His!"

111. Kim B. Clark, "Identity and Purpose in God's Eternal Plan" Brigham Young University–Idaho devotional, Apr. 22, 2014), byui.edu.

Appendix A: A Dream

Mark: I once had a dream in which I was sitting in an unfamiliar home, waiting for someone. Unfamiliar people were around me working at desks. Suddenly, a smiling little girl (maybe three years old) with curly black hair and big brown eyes poked her head around the corner, pointed at me, and enthusiastically announced, "Today is your birthday!" Just as fast as she had come, she disappeared back around the corner.

I wondered how she knew that, and I was a little embarrassed she would say it so loudly, although no one seemed to hear. While I was wondering, she suddenly popped out again and gestured with her hands waving above her head, singing at the top of her lungs, "Heavenly Father"—long pause while holding the note on the word *Father*—"made it your birthday today!"

She vanished again. I glanced around, a bit self-conscious, but everyone was still working, not paying attention to or noticing this little performance. I smiled to myself, feeling appreciation for the special, kind attention she gave me.

Then I thought, "It's true! How sweet she would somehow know that not only is today my birthday, but my birth and every birth is a glorious gift from Heavenly Father and part of His plan, whether anyone else knows about it or not."

Then I awoke and realized that it was indeed my birthday.

This dream came to me at a time when I was feeling discouraged in writing this book, and it motivated me to press on. It emphasized the idea that each physical birth is part of God's plan, pivotal and important, wisely planned, lovingly given, and directed by God.

Appendix B: Gospel-Centered Affirmations

Mark: As a ward in Biloxi, Mississippi, we made a video of the below affirmations, taking turns speaking the parts in sequence. We hoped the video would show our shared equality in divine birthright and identity. Those who participated included ward members from all stages and walks of life.

Perhaps occasionally reviewing affirmations on divine identity can provide a way to remind ourselves of who we are, especially when we need a boost from time to time. Affirmations can come in the form of short self-written statements, hymns, scriptures, quotes, and so forth.

Here are some examples of gospel-centered affirmations:

- I am a spirit child of Heavenly Father and Heavenly Mother. As the offspring of God, I have the potential to become like them.
- "I am a son [or daughter] of God, in the similitude of his Only Begotten" (Moses 1:13).
- As their child, I have, "a divine nature and destiny,"[112] including spiritual gifts (see Doctrine and Covenants 46:11), purpose, and work.
- I am so beloved by my heavenly parents and my Savior that, along with all mankind, I am the reason for the plan of salvation, the Creation, the Fall, and even the Atonement with all of its incomprehensible suffering and sacrifice. I am that important to them.
- "For behold, this is my work and my glory, to bring to pass the immortality and eternal life of man" (Moses 1:39).
- "For God so loved the world, that he gave his only begotten Son, that whosoever believeth in him should not perish, but have everlasting life" (John 3:16).
- I chose my Father's plan in the world before I was born. Despite great opposition, I covenanted to follow the Lord Jesus Christ

112. "The Family: A Proclamation to the World," ChurchofJesusChrist.org.

and to sustain Him in His missions of Creation, Atonement, and Judgment.

- "I am a disciple of Jesus Christ, the Son of God. I have been called of him to declare his word among his people, that they might have everlasting life" (3 Nephi 5:13).
- If faithful, I will inherit all things as a joint heir with my Brother, the Lord Jesus Christ.
- "If children, then heirs; heirs of God, and joint-heirs with Christ" (Romans 8:17). "[They] that overcometh shall inherit all things; and I will be [their] God, and [they] shall be my [children]" (Revelation 21:7).
- I am a covenant member of The Church of Jesus Christ of Latter-day Saints. I belong to and am needed in His kingdom. As a member, I have an important role to play, just like parts of the human body all have important roles (see 1 Corinthians 12:12–27). Through these covenants, I belong to an eternal family wherein I likewise have important, essential belonging and work to do, including family history and temple work.
- I am developing His characteristics as I follow His plan and receive His ordinances in meekness and faith. By following this plan, I can and do receive the greatest possible peace, joy, knowledge, and power for good in this life and in the world to come.
- I have the power to do all things the Lord has commanded me. I cannot comprehend all things now or be perfect now, but I trust in Him with faith. I believe He is perfect and can comprehend all things.
- "I know that the Lord giveth no commandments unto the children of men, save he shall prepare a way for them that they may accomplish the thing which he commandeth them" (1 Nephi 3:7).
- My body is a sacred gift from God, made in the image of the physical bodies of my heavenly parents. I will be resurrected and receive a perfect immortal body as a gift from Jesus Christ, just like He was resurrected when He broke the bands of physical death (see Matthew 28:6–7).
- My patriarchal blessing helps me know who I am by declaring

my lineage in the house of Israel and by giving me insights into my person, character, strengths, and mission on earth. This is who I am.

- I am not defined by my weakness or mistakes. I have weakness and make mistakes partly because that is His plan for me. These things encourage me to have meekness, be humble, repent, and exercise faith in my Redeemer.
- "If men come unto me I will show unto them their weakness. I give unto men weakness that they may be humble; and my grace is sufficient for all men that humble themselves before me; for if they humble themselves before me, and have faith in me, then will I make weak things become strong unto them" (Ether 12:27).
- I am not defined by comparison to others.
- "[My] contest is not with [others] but with [myself]."[113] God "cheers on *every* runner, calling out that the race is against sin, *not* against each other."[114]
- I value the things of eternity over the things of the world. I am on the Lord's team, which will win, destroying all wickedness.
- "This latter-day work will destroy the powers of darkness and bring about the salvation of the human family."[115]
- "I am a child of God, and He has sent me here."[116]
- "Learn for yourselves who you really are. Ask your Heavenly Father, in the name of Jesus Christ, how He feels about you and your mission here on earth. If you ask with real intent, over time the Spirit will whisper the life-changing truth to you."[117]

---

113. Boyd K. Packer, *That All May Be Edified* (Salt Lake City: Bookcraft, 1982), 51–52.
114. Jeffrey R. Holland, "The Other Prodigal," *Ensign*, May 2002, 64.
115. David A. Bednar, "Let This House Be Built Unto My Name," *Ensign* or *Liahona*, May 2020, 87.
116. "I Am a Child of God," *Hymns*, no. 301.
117. Russell M. Nelson, "Stand as True Millennials," *Ensign*, Oct. 2016.

Appendix C: Advice for Understanding Identity

We hesitate to become specific in recommending how to implement the understanding of divine identity into our lives generally. We feel we are struggling to do this ourselves. Perhaps by discussing these issues with loved ones and together, even on social media, we can help one another find individualized solutions to our personal circumstances and challenges.

Nevertheless, it seems that some general principles apply to us all. In our experience, much of the struggle in understanding divine identity surrounds false beliefs. Elder Lawrence E. Corbridge clearly explains this important concept in the following quote:

> Most of us act based on our beliefs, especially what we believe to be in our self-interest. The problem is, we are sometimes wrong.
>
> Someone may believe in God and that pornography is wrong and yet still click on a site wrongly believing that he will be happier if he does or he can't help but not click or it isn't hurting anyone else and it is not that bad. He is just wrong.
>
> Someone may believe it is wrong to lie and yet lie on occasion, wrongly believing he will be better off if the truth is not known. He is just wrong.
>
> Someone may believe and even know that Jesus is the Christ and still deny Him not once but three times because of the mistaken belief that he would be better off appeasing the crowd. Peter wasn't evil. I am not even sure he was weak. He was just wrong.
>
> When you act badly, you may think you are bad, when in truth you are usually mistaken. You are just wrong. The challenge is not so much closing the gap between our actions and our beliefs; rather, the challenge is closing the gap between our beliefs and the truth. That is the challenge.[118]

---

118. Lawrence E. Corbridge, "Stand Forever," Brigham Young University Devotional Address, Jan.22, 2019.

We might falsely believe that understanding divine identity is not worth trying to do because it is incomprehensible anyway. We might falsely believe that science must be right about our origin in every respect, that religion and science are incompatible, or that there is no place for a religious perspective on identity. We might falsely believe that distractions such as media are harmless to our understanding divine identity. We might falsely believe that withdrawing from the difficult fight of understanding identity will make us happier.

We might falsely believe that our weaknesses or strengths, our failures or successes, form our true identity. If we are not careful, strength and success can lead to pride, a condition that confuses identity in epic proportions, as we witness in Lucifer and his followers.[119] Weakness and imperfection do not define us, but they can help us understand our identity better, partly because weakness helps humble us and turn us to God, over and over again. "And if men come unto me I will show unto them their weakness. I give unto men weakness that they may be humble; and my grace is sufficient for all men that humble themselves before me" (Ether 12:27).

The words *give* and *gift* are related and have similar meanings and origins. "I give unto men weakness," God says. Our weakness in mortality can correctly be seen as a gift from the Lord because weakness has the power to turn us earnestly to Him. Weakness encourages meekness and humility, which nurtures faith and repentance, which subsequently allows for His grace and our divine destiny. "And again, behold I say unto you that he cannot have faith and hope, save he shall be meek, and lowly of heart" (Moroni 7:43). When positioned in gospel sequence, weakness assumes an important place in understanding our identity and realizing our divine destiny.

---

119. As we see so clearly in Satan's catastrophic and dramatic fall, pride obscures and confuses identity. Note how many times in the following scriptures Satan proudly refers to himself as he rejects God's plan for His children. "That Satan . . . is the same which was from the beginning, and he came before me, saying—Behold, here am I, send me, I will be thy son, and I will redeem all mankind, that one soul shall not be lost, and surely I will do it; wherefore give me thine honor" (Moses 4:1; see also Isaiah 14:12–15). Satan had an "I" problem. In his pride and resulting confusion, he couldn't see himself clearly. He therefore tried to destroy the identity of all God's children by rejecting God's designs for us. He is still trying to do this.

It is difficult to understand our amazing divine identity, let alone accept, remember, and realize it. Weakness, pride, the teachings of the secular world, disease, distractions, fear, and laziness can all make understanding identity even more difficult. In the next life, our identity will become clear to us. "For now we see through a glass, darkly; but then face to face: now I know in part; but then shall I know even as also I am known" (1 Corinthians 13:12).

For now, the Lord in His wisdom has given us many challenging conditions in mortality. These include incomprehensible truths, weakness, a veil of forgetfulness, a physical body, unfairness, the mists of darkness, abundant distractions, and unpredictable circumstances. The challenge of knowing who we really are is great, but the blessings of trying are even greater.

Perhaps the most important stepping stones to understanding divine identity are simply studying it carefully, counseling together, and praying about it earnestly. Keeping the regular devotions of scripture study, prayer, church attendance, temple worship, repentance, and faithful service will of course greatly help with any spiritual challenge.

Meditation, care for our bodies and minds, healthy connection with trusted friends and leaders, reviewing gospel affirmations of identity, avoiding distractions, turning to our patriarchal blessings, and surrounding ourselves with uplifting music, pictures, and decor can all help us accept and remember our divine identity. Even spending time in nature witnessing our place among His creations—standing in awe of God's amazing creativity and learning from the celestial obedience of God's handiwork (see Doctrine and Covenants 88:25)—can be of great help. To paraphrase Henry David Thoreau, get lost in nature and you will find yourself.

In particular, we have found power to understand divine identity in missionary work, family history, and temple work. It seems that any time we focus on helping someone make and keep sacred covenants, we are becoming who we are designed to become and helping others do the same. There is special power in these activities because they are at the very core of our divine identity and destiny.

Appendix D: Central Concepts Found in This Book

- Our identity can be traced to our origins (p. 11).
- We are offspring, not accidents (p. 13).
- Weakness, adversity, and opposition in mortality do not define us—they define our mortal condition (p. 14).
- God's matchless gift of life is always packaged together with His greatest gifts of love (p. 17).
- As children of heavenly parents, and as Adam and Eve's offspring, we are here by covenant, not by accident (p. 42).
- An important part of understanding the phrase "children of the covenant" is that we are the children of righteous, covenant ancestors. We belong to them and they to us. Understanding identity starts with understanding our covenant origins (p. 44).
- We are born needy, but as children of the covenant, we are also born needed (p. 45).
- If you have trouble believing in miracles, maybe start with this: you are a miracle (p. 52).
- The Heavenly King offers us covenants to claim our royal birthright as His offspring (p. 62).
- Covenants are the means God utilizes to turn divine identity into divine destiny (p. 64).
- The degree to which we embrace Jesus Christ and His gift of daily repentance is the degree to which we will understand, remember, and realize our divine identity (p. 69).
- When we seek charity, the pure love of Christ, we are pursuing the very center of His identity and our destiny (p. 71).
- The covenants inherently tie our identity to our work and our work to our destiny (p. 73).
- It is in exaltation that our identity is made complete and becomes our destiny (p. 78).

- Through Jesus Christ, we begin with divine but vulnerable identity and end with divine and everlasting destiny (p. 81).
- Based on Jesus's identity and ours, He asks us to love and to believe in Him, to love and to believe in ourselves, and to love and to believe in each other (p. 84).
- We cannot understand our divine identity until we understand the identity of Jesus Christ (p. 86).
- Understanding divine identity is understanding reality (p. 87).
- As God's children, we are not designed to compete with each other. We are designed to cooperate with each other (p. 89).
- Divine identity is a great destroyer of pride and equalizer of humanity (p. 89).
- It is only through Jesus Christ that we are truly and completely defined (p. 90).

President Henry B. Eyring said, "What will matter most is what [others] learn from [you] about who they really are and what they can really become. My guess is that they won't learn it so much from lectures. They will get it from feelings of who you are, who you think they are, and what you think they might become."[120]

120. Henry B. Eyring, "Teaching Is a Moral Act" (Brigham Young University devotional, Aug. 27, 1991), 3, speeches.byu.edu.

About the Authors

Authors Mark and Sarah are father and daughter.

Dr. Mark D. Lyman, MD, is a physician board certified in both clinical and anatomic pathology. Career military, Mark is a colonel in the United States Air Force. He has deployed as a flight surgeon with his KC-135 air refueling squadron to Saudi Arabia for Operation Southern Watch and to Spain in support of the Kosovo Conflict where he flew in combat missions. By general officer appointment, he serves as the Air Force Consultant to the Surgeon General for Pathology.

As a scientist, Mark is published in peer-reviewed medical literature on recurrent T-cell acute lymphoblastic leukemia/lymphoma, but his first book publication (2020) is *Love, Kynra*, a biography available on Amazon. *I Am His* is Mark's first gospel-centered book, and he is close to completing a sequel. Also gospel-centered, Mark's short story on the covenant path titled "Streetlights in the Snow" has been accepted for publication in the *Liahona*.

In his spare time, Mark enjoys raising chickens, doing family history, baking sourdough, swimming long distances, and wearing Crocs in slip-on mode while playing knockout against his posterity. He and his loving wife, Brenda, are the adoring parents of six beautiful children and two precious grandchildren. They reside in Falls Church City, Virginia.

Sarah L. Lyman is a business professional with an MBA from Brigham Young University. She has worked with both startups and Fortune 500 companies as a management consultant and internal strategist. In her studies, she received the Bateman Scholar Award (2018) and the Hawes Scholar Award (2023).

Outside of work, she assisted her dad as editor, contributor, and audiobook voice for *Love, Kynra*. She is currently coauthoring a collaborative book regarding the role of women in the gospel of Jesus Christ with three amazing friends. Sarah enjoys hiking mountains, exploring Europe, perusing most any museum, drinking hot chocolate year-round, and holding any baby that needs to take a nap. She currently resides in Washington D.C. with her husband, Isaac Smith.